D1371543

FEMININE
GYMNASTICS
2nd edition

by

PHYLLIS COOPER

illustrated by
A. BRUCE FREDERICK

Burgess Publishing Company
Minneapolis, Minnesota

5   6   7   8   9   0

Preface

Feminine Gymnastics was written to serve as a guide for teachers and coaches of gymnastics in the school, club, and other organizations. The material covered provides the instructor with methods of teaching, subjective and objective methods of evaluating, skill analysis, spotting techniques, and common errors that are made when students perform the skills for the first time. Safety is of utmost importance and is stressed constantly throughout the text.

Suggestions for class procedures and program planning have been included with the hope that they will serve as guidelines when creating or designing a program to fit the needs of your particular school or club.

The area of competitive gymnastics is also discussed, along with judging techniques and instructions on running a gymnastic meet.

Gymnastics is fast becoming a very popular sport for both participants and spectators, and there is no doubt as to the values this activity offers each individual.

I wish to acknowledge Bruce Frederick for his outstanding illustrations; to Mark S. Mock and Film Makers of Philadelphia for filming the skills used for the illustrations; and to the George Nissen Company for allowing me to use their equipment diagrams.

Phyllis Cooper

To The Reader

Many of the skills have been described to one side (*e.g.,* left foot or left hand leading). To perform the skill to the other side, reverse the directions for movement of the hands or feet.

For spotting the *inside hand* (near) is the one closest to the performer, and the *outside hand* (far) is the one away from the performer. If the spotter is standing directly beside a performer, the inside hand is the hand closest to the part of the body that initiates the movement. There are also other spotting methods for each skill, but the one(s) presented have been proven very successful by the author.

The code used throughout the book is as follows:

PT	Performance technique
SP	Spotting Technique
CE	Common errors made by beginners
MO	Movements out of the skill described
VA	Variations of the skill
POB	Position on bed of trampoline

Each group of skills has been described in a general order of progression. However, this is not the only progression that can or should be used because individuals and groups of individuals tend to have varied capacities for learning.

A Philosophy

In life generally those things that are built on a solid foundation will last longer, and the final results or outcomes can be more productive and rewarding. Building a strong foundation in gymnastics begins by learning the fundamental skills well so they may be executed efficiently. When this is done, success comes often and frustration seldom occurs.

It is important to know where the body is at all times in relation to space (kinesthetic sense) from the very beginning in gymnastics. Some people are gifted with a great amount of kinesthetic awareness, while others must learn every step of the way. Therefore, it is essential for a student to feel her body in motion on the mat (e.g., doing a forward roll) before attempting motion in the air without support of the hands or feet.

As we look around us, we see individuals of many shapes and sizes. Some are strong, some weak; some flexible, some not so flexible; some are agile, while others move a bit slower; and some have more interest and drive than others. All of these individuals cannot excel in gymnastics, but all can have success to some degree at some level. As you teach the sport, keep in mind that everyone in a given group can do only what her mind and body will allow, and she should be evaluated accordingly.

Contents

List Of Illustrations

TRAMPOLINE SKILLS (Figures 313-344)

CHAPTER ONE
LOCOMOTOR SKILLS

"Why Locomotor Skills In Gymnastics?"

We learn to walk when we are about a year old. We get a helping hand only when we fall, and as soon as we prove ourselves proficient, everyone seems to take it for granted that no more need be said about our locomotor skills. As we get more daring, we try our luck at running and begin to imitate older playmates as they hop, skip, and jump. Some individuals are fortunate enough to develop those locomotor skills during childhood; however, too often boys and girls go through twelve years of school without learning the basic locomotor skills essential to efficient movement.

Why do we need these skills in a gymnastics book? A gymnast, like any other athlete, can perform more gracefully and efficiently with a good background in basic movement, and for a gymnast, locomotor skills are an integral part of floor exercise and balance beam routine composition. Learning to run well is a must for any individual who wishes to become a good vaulter because the efficiency and speed of the run greatly influence the execution of the vault. If proper technique of basic locomotor skills is taught, then gymnasts can execute skills more gracefully and efficiently.

The basic locomotor skills include walking, running, hopping, skipping, jumping, leaping, sliding and galloping. The proper techniques of these skills and variations used specifically for gymnastics will be described.

Note: Refer to dance section of chapter III for description of ballet arm and leg positions.

WALKS

Walking in gymnastic exercises is different from general everyday walking. The "dance walk," which is performed with the legs turned slightly out from the hips and the toe rather than the heel leading is used. Walks should be performed lightly and fluidly, with the entire body erect. The shoulders must be relaxed for aesthetic appearance and good body lines. The arms should hold a definite position, with the index finger an extension of the arm. Abdominal and gluteal muscles should be tense, never allowing the hips to protrude backward. Small steps are more appropriate for gymnastics.

VARIATIONS FOR PRACTICE aid in developing confidence, balance control, and awareness of body positions in motion.

1. Arms out to sides, palms down. Walk on line on floor. Do not allow body to be rigid. Eyes spot stationary object at eye level in front of body.
2. Start with both arms out to sides of body and parallel to floor. As left foot moves forward, bring right arm to front of body (parallel to floor) leading with inside of wrist. As right foot moves forward, move right arm out to side position leading with back of wrist; slight bend in elbow. (Fig. 1)
3. Repeat #2 moving left arm.
4. Arms out to sides; walk on balls of feet with very little knee bend. (Fig. 2)

1

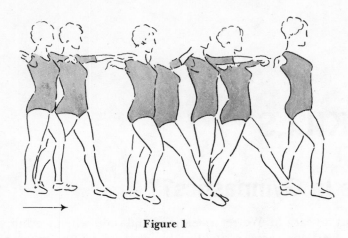

Figure 1

Figure 2

5. Arms out to sides and parallel to floor; step onto right foot bending right knee. Step onto left foot on ball of foot, then step onto ball of right foot (low, high, high). On the low steps, the foot should be turned slightly out with the heel turned in. (Fig. 3)
6. Repeat #5 starting low step on left foot.
7. Arms out to side and make steps (high, low, low).
8. Walk backwards; be careful not to lean forward.
9. Walk on a diagonal; keeping upper body forward. (Fig. 4)
10. Walk to music.
11. Transfer walks to balance beam.

Figure 3

Figure 4

RUNS

Learning to run gracefully requires many hours of concentrated practice. The beginner must run low and slowly at first and gradually increase the height and speed.

The stride should be even, and the movement should be smooth and free. The arms should swing naturally in opposition to the legs; never allow them to cross in front or in back of the body. The shoulders should be in a forward position, and the head should be held in a natural position. Never let the upper body sag forward; the entire body should lean slightly forward.

Forward momentum is created by full leg, ankle, and hip extension. When the back leg extends and moves to become the forward leg, it lands with a bent knee; then the ball of the foot pushes down and back on the floor, resulting in full extension of that leg. The last part of the foot to leave the floor and the first part to contact the floor should be the ball. The heels should not come in complete contact with the floor.

VARIATIONS FOR PRACTICE

1. Run in a straight line, first slow and then fast.
2. Run in a semicircle to the right. Lean slightly into the center of the semicircle mostly with shoulders and head. (Fig. 5)

Figure 5

3. Repeat #2 running to the left; reverse arms.
4. Run to music.
5. Transfer running in a straight line to the balance beam.

HOPS

A hop is the removal of weight from one foot and its return to the same foot; it is usually preceded by another locomotor skill, such as a walk (step). On the hop, the right leg is lifted in front of the body with the knee bent and the upper part of the leg parallel to the floor. The knee should be turned out and the heel turned in (closer to the midline of the body than the knee, but forward of the knee). The left leg starts in the bent-knee position; the toes point toward the floor as the foot leaves the floor to push the entire body upward. For maximum height the head and chest must also be lifted. The arms may move in opposition to the legs, may be in third position or may be held sideways. (Fig. 6)

Figure 6

1. Take a step. Lift one leg and extend it sideways. As the other leg pushes off the floor, the knee will turn outward and bend, allowing the foot to contact the buttocks. Hold arms sideways. (Fig. 7)

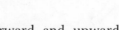

Figure 7

2. Perform #1 but extend one leg forward and upward rather than to the side. (Fig. 8).
3. Hop to music.

Figure 8

SKIPS

The skip is a combination of the step and the hop. It has an uneven rhythm. The step and hop are executed on the same foot. Refer to description of the hop for details of arm and body positions. Precede hop with step for skip.

JUMPS

The jump is a spring from one or two feet and a landing on both feet. The main purposes of jumps are to gain height or distance. If height is the main objective, the movement must go up and down in the same vertical plane. If the main objective is distance, then the center of gravity must be displaced to afford forward momentum. Arm and body positions will vary with the different types of jumps. Jumps should be explosive movements.

VARIATIONS FOR PRACTICE

1. *Squat jump* (Fig. 9)
   Hold arms sideways, stand with feet close together with one foot slightly in front of the other. Bend knees (go into semi-plié position) and immediately spring upward lifting the heels to the buttocks. Lower the legs (extend) before landing, and make sure the landing is in a semi-plié position for balance and to absorb shock. The head and chest should be lifted for added height. Try to make the jump and landing in the same vertical plane to avoid loss of balance.

Figure 9

2. *Tuck jump* (Fig. 10)

The same principles of movement involved in the squat jump are used in the tuck jump. The only difference is the position of the legs. Instead of being lifted to the buttocks as in figure 9, the knees are brought to the chest.

Figure 10

3. *"C" or Cheerleading jump* (Fig. 11)

The "C" jump is performed in a vertical plane. Start in standing position; slightly bend knees and spring vertically. As the feet leave the floor, lift them back and up toward the head; at the same time, arch the back, tilt the head backward, and move the arms upward and backward. Return to original position upon landing.

Figure 11

4. *Straddle jump* (Fig. 12)

Keep upper body erect at all times. After springing upward from floor, lift legs sideways and upward in a wide straddle position. Move arms sideways to touch toes. Bring legs together before landing.

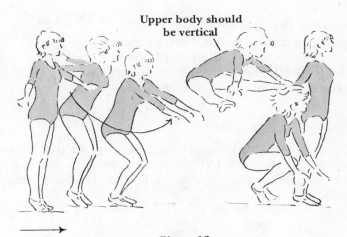

Upper body should be vertical

Figure 12

5. *Arch jump* (Fig. 13-14)

The arch *jump* is used mainly to achieve distance; however, it is sometimes used to gain height.

Distance

From a stand, go ino a bent-knee position and simultaneously move the arms to a backupward position (palms up). The hips are directly over the feet, and the *shoulders are forward of the knees and feet.* (Fig. 13)

Figure 13

Height

Arms move same as above. When the bent knee position is attained, the *shoulders should be directly over the feet*; maintain that relationship throughout the jump. (Fig. 14)

PRACTICE HINTS FOR JUMPS

1. Start jumps low; then gradually increase height.
2. Make all jumps appear explosive.
3. Practice a couple of jumps in succession.
4. Make sure to use arms to assist in gaining height.
5. Transfer squat, arch, and tuck jumps to balance beam.
6. Other jumps can be incorporated in floor exercise.

Figure 14

LEAPS

Leaps are slower than a run because they involve height and distance. As the transference of weight from one foot to the other is made, the body is completely suspended in air. Height and distance are attained as a result of a very strong downbackward push from the back leg, which starts in a bent leg position. As the back leg extends and the front leg reaches forward and up, the head and chest are strongly lifted. Arms are held in opposition to the legs. The leap should be a very explosive movement.

VARIATIONS FOR PRACTICE

1. Run, run, leap, run, run, leap. (l = left foot, r = right foot) l r l r l r
2. Practice over a low object such as a bench or beam; the object should be at least twelve inches off the floor. This technique will force the performer to get off the floor and to lift the back leg and delay lowering it.

LEAP VARIATIONS

1. *Step-push leap—step sissone* (Fig. 15)
   Step forward on right foot and slide left foot to meet right (feet almost in fifth position after step). Bend knees, push with back (left) foot upward. Land on forward foot. Keep arms in opposition or to side of body parallel to floor.

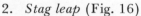

Figure 15

2. *Stag leap* (Fig. 16)
   As the leap is initiated by the back (right) leg, the forward (left) leg extends foreupward. Immediately bend left knee and touch left toe to right knee. Land on left foot. Keep arms in opposition to legs or in second position (sideways). Lift the head and chest.

Figure 16

3. *Split leap* (Fig. 17)

After the back leg initiates the foreupward movement of the body, one leg reaches forward while the other leg reaches backward and upward to an even split position. Lift the head and chest and allow the back to arch slightly. Land on forward foot with slight knee bend. When left leg is forward, hold right arm obliquely forward and left arm in second position. (Fig. 17)

Figure 17

4. *Scissors leap (preceded by a run)* (Fig. 18)

Take off on the left foot, extending the right leg forward. While suspended, switch legs so that the right leg becomes the back leg and lift head and chest. Land on left foot. Keep arms to side (second position).

Figure 18

GALLOP (Left foot leading) (Fig. 19)

A gallop is a step, close movement with uneven rhythm. The original forward foot is always in the lead. Height is gained as the push-off is made from the front foot.

Step forward onto bent leg and transfer weight to that foot. Draw the back foot behind the front foot while the front leg is extending (on toe). Quickly shift the weight to the back leg while lifting the front leg forward to prepare for the next step.

Always hold the upper body and head erect. The arms may be held sideways or obliquely backward.

Figure 19

VARIATIONS FOR PRACTICE

1. Step, close, step, hesitate and bring back leg forward and step, close, step.
   l r l   r l r
2. Practice to music.
3. Transfer to balance beam.

SLIDE

A slide is a step, close with uneven rhythm and is usually performed sideways or on a diagonal. The same principles of movement involved in the gallop are involved in the slide, but the body moves sideways. Hold arms sideward. The body is always slightly behind the lead foot.

VARIATIONS FOR PRACTICE

1. Step, close, step, half hop pivot turn, step, close, step. (Fig. 20)
   l r l   l   r l r
2. Slide on a diagonal.
3. Slide to music.
4. Transfer movement to floor exercise routine and balance beam.

Figure 20

Teaching Suggestions

The atmosphere for introducing this type of activity is very important. Most girls are inhibited when wearing leotards (if used) for the first time. There must be good rapport with the students and respect by students for teacher and by teacher for students. Since this type of activity is usually not covered in physical education classes, there will be many unexpected giggles and awkward movements that the teacher must accept. Eventually, students will no longer find hopping or leaping around the gym unusual.

SUGGESTED FORMAT

1. Have very low background music.
2. Have group spaced on floor (sitting while talking) to allow freedom of movement.
3. Discuss unit plan.
4. Describe first skill (usually the walk) and demonstrate (or have demonstrated).
5. Immediately involve the entire class in performing the skill (so they won't have too much time to think about becoming "wall flowers").
6. Compliment the group and review the skill, pointing out mistakes made but not directing comments to any individual. Sometimes it helps to mock the mistakes in an exaggerated form since students often like to see the teacher being one of the gang.
7. Have one quarter of the class perform at a time while the others watch.
8. Use music and play follow the leader, with you (the teacher) being the leader. Decide on a floor pattern before class or improvise.
   Example: Moving in a single file around the gym, make a diagram similar to the one below.

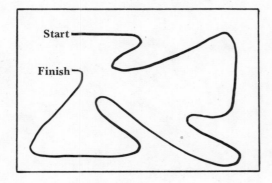

Variations can be incorporated, such as low and high walks and walking backwards. Be prepared for a possible jam-up!

9. Review two more skills, such as the step hop and slide. Practice each a few times, then combine them in a simple manner, such as four walks, four step hops and four slides. Perform in small groups to music. Have the groups work in a straight line, on a diagonal, or in a circle.
   Sometimes it helps to make a contest out of this activity, such as "Which group is the most synchronized?"
10. After all skills are covered, have students move the way they "feel" to the music, combining the skills and adding turns. Expect anything from an empty floor until a "brave soul" makes the first move to patterns involving only one skill such as walks or turns.

Note: Commercial records made especially for locomotor skills or dance moves can be purchased. If this is not possible, then music such as "Alley Cat" or any similar record with an even rhythm can be used for walks, runs, skips, and fast slides and gallops.

NOTES

CHAPTER TWO
TUMBLING AND ACROBATIC SKILLS

The values of tumbling in the physical education program are numerous. This type of activity challenges students to compete against themselves, as they do not have a teammate to help them maneuver their bodies through some of the intricate skills (except as a spotter). Tumbling and acrobatic skills, along with single and dual stunts, help coordination, flexibility, balance, strength, self-confidence, agility, kinesthetic perception, courage, and rhythm or timing.

If students are given a strong program in basic tumbling skills and are required to master those skills, their chances for success on apparatus will be greater because movements learned in tumbling can be transferred to other activities.

It is essential to have a definite skill progression for each group or individual and to have students master the fundamental skills before attempting more difficult ones. The following is a list of skills to be covered in this chapter. They are listed in a suggested progression sequence; however, other progressions may be used, depending on the ability level and size of the group.

The suggested progression is as follows:

Tripod	Valdez
Tip-up	Hurdle
Headstand	Round-off
Forward roll with variations	Kip
Handstand kick-up	Headspring
Backward roll with variations	Handspring
Dive roll	Front handspring with variations
Handstand forward roll	Tinsica
Handstand chest roll	Back handspring with variations
Cartwheel with variations	Side aerial
Back roll extension	Front aerial
Mule kick (snap down)	Back flip
Limbre	Round-off back sommie
Back walkover with variations	Round-off back layout
Front Walkover with variations	Round-off full twist

In order to coordinate the spotting techniques and variations, skills are not described in the exact order. Some of the skills are oriented to the left or right. To perform the skills to the other side, reverse the directions. The code used in descriptions of the skills is on page v.

Special Conditioning Exercises

TUCK JUMPS IN SUCCESSION

Purpose: To develop explosive power in the legs.
Technique: Spring vertically; bring knees to chest. Grasp ankles or hold legs around knees while suspended. Extend legs before landing.

STRETCH IN STRADDLE POSITION

Purpose: To develop flexibility in hamstrings and lower back.
Technique: Sit in wide straddle position; tilt pelvic area forward. Bend forward over knee, leading with chest; keep head up and arms back. Hold *or* bounce over right leg for eight counts. Hold *or* bounce between legs for eight counts. Hold *or* bounce over left leg for eight counts.
Variations: 1. Do not tilt pelvis; have arms overhead; round the back and reach forward trying to touch the head to the knees.
2. With partner: Face each other sitting in a wide straddle position with soles of feet together; push and pull each other, trying to place upper body flat on floor when going forward and when going backward.

KNEES TO NOSE ON BACK

Purpose: To stretch hamstrings and Achilles' tendon.
Technique: From supine position, lift legs (straight and together) and hips overhead to touch toes on mat behind head. Rest arms on floor at sides of body. Maintain straight knees, flex and extend ankles.
Variation: Grasp toes and pull legs closer to body.

PUSH-UPS

Purpose: To develop strength in triceps, rhomboids, and flexors and extensors in the forearm.
Technique: In a prone position place hands just under shoulders with fingers pointing forward. Curl toes under feet and extend arms, keeping entire body straight. Do not allow the hips to sag or to extend upward. Bend elbows, lowering body and allow chin to touch floor; extend arms so that body is pushed to the original position.

BACKBEND (bridge)

Purpose: To develop flexibility in the shoulders and lower back.
Technique: From a supine position on the mat, place the heels as close to the hips as possible. Place hands on mat at each side of neck (under shoulders) with fingers pointing toward feet. Extend arms and legs (look at fingers) and push body into arched position. It is very important to keep the arms straight. Rock backwards and forwards trying to force the shoulders forward of the hands.
Hint: Work with partner to learn. Partner assists performer in getting to arched position and aids with rocking motion. Partner should stand in front of performer (between legs) with one foot in front of the other. Place hands on lower back and upper hip area.
Variations: 1. Walk in backbend position.
2. Extend legs alternately to 90° while walking in backbend.
3. Go into backbend from standing position; hop from hands to feet.
4. Keep legs together and straight with feet flat on mat and push shoulders forward.
5. Touch toes then go to back bend position from stand.

SPLITS (do to both sides)

Purpose: To develop flexibility of the hamstrings and inner thigh muscles and to develop good split positions.
Technique: Standing on mat, step forward on right foot and turn left foot toward left side of body (similar to lunge position). Turn upper body toward forward foot and slide left foot back as far as possible. To learn, use the hands by placing them on the mat to the side of the body and force the body a little closer to the mat on each attempt.
Hint: Sometimes it is better to do this exercise on the floor to enable feet to slide freely.
Keep hips and shoulders square at all times.

Variations: 1. Stand with back to wall or some other flat surface. Bend forward and extend one leg up the wall. Force body as close to wall as possible with legs in split position.
2. Stand with back to wall, heel of one foot touching wall. Have partner pick up other leg and try to lift it gradually to touch wall behind shoulder.

RUNNING (in place or laps around the gym)

Purpose: To develop or strengthen flexors and extensors of legs. To stimulate circulatory system. To develop endurance.

LEG LIFTS

Purpose: To develop strength in abdominals, hip flexors, and lower back muscles.
Technique: Lie on mat in supine position, keeping small of back on mat. Lift legs (straight and together) about five inches off the mat, and move them into a wide straddle position; then return to starting position and lower to the mat. Repeat without resting.

Safety Hints

1. Never allow students to tumble unless supervised.
2. Always tumble on mats.
3. Performers in a group should always work in the same direction to avoid collisions.
4. While others are performing, stay clear of the mats unless you are acting as a spotter.
5. Remove all jewelry before tumbling.
6. Keep mats clean and in good condition. Avoid tumbling on mats with tears or mats covered with any type of dust.
7. Use safety devices when necessary, e.g., spotting belts.
8. If mats are to be used in succession, they should be secured with tape, rope, or some other material that will keep them from slipping apart.
9. It is advisable to have student assistants if possible. Those girls should be given special instruction (before or after school) on correct spotting techniques.
10. Remind students that they should complete the skill being attempted and not "chicken out" in the middle of the skill.
11. Students should *not* be allowed to "goof off" at any time.
12. Advise students to *keep eyes open at all times* to develop kinesthetic awareness and to help prevent accidents.
13. Students should not tumble when fatigued.
14. Have a definite skill progression.

Lead-up Skills

Before learning tumbling and acrobatic skills there are certain skills a student should master. These skills will help develop a better body awareness in space; they are skills that almost everyone can do with little effort.

TRIPOD (Fig. 21)

PT From kneeling position place hands on mat at least shoulder width apart. Bend elbows and spread fingers apart. Place head on mat forward of the hands to form a triangular base. Lift hips upward by extending the legs and place one knee at a time on the elbows. Point toes toward ceiling. Hold for three seconds, and then come down one leg at a time.

Figure   21

SP Place one hand on back of neck and the other hand on the legs.

CE
1. Triangle (base) too small or too large.
2. Top of head rather than area of hairline on mat.
3. Elbows not stable while inverted. (Think about forcing them toward each other.)
4. Trying to jump into position rather than controlling the leg lift.

TIP-UP (Fig. 22)

PT From squat position with knees apart, place hands on mat between legs (fingers spread apart). Press knees forcefully against elbows, which are slightly bent, and shift body weight to hands. Keep head up. Hold for three seconds and then return to squat position.

SP Kneel beside performer and assist by supporting shoulder and back of thigh.

CE
1. Arms not slightly bent.
2. Knees too far apart or too close.
3. Failure to keep head up.
4. Failure to elevate hips before tipping forward.
5. Failure to squeeze knees against elbows forcefully.

Figure 22

HEADSTAND (Fig. 23)

PT *From tripod,* slightly arch back and bring knees together. Extend legs slowly to an inverted position while slowly shifting hips forward so that body will have a slight arch. Hold for three seconds, reverse precedure, and return to tripod.

SP For all variations of headstand: Stand to side of performer and assist with balance by grasping legs just above the knee or at the ankle.

CE
1. Top of head rather than hairline area on mat.
2. Not allowing back to slightly arch.
3. Not keeping calf and thigh muscles tense.
4. Allowing arms to collapse or wobble.
5. Insufficient base of support (triangle).

Figure 23

PT *From prone position* (Fig. 24), lift hips to allow hands and head to form triangle on mat. Draw (or walk) hips to an overhead position. When hips are over head, lift both legs (together and straight) to an inverted position while slightly arching the back. Keep calf and thigh muscles taut.

CE
1. Same as 1-4 from tripod position.
2. Failure to lift hips to an overhead position before extending legs vertically.

Figure 24

PT *Kick-up* (Fig. 25). From squat or lunge position, form a triangle with the head and hands. Draw one leg close to the chest, extend other leg to the rear. Lift the extended leg to an inverted position while pushing with the bent leg. Bring both legs together in the inverted position; extend body with a slight arch in the back. Hold three seconds and return to the mat, one leg at a time.

CE 1. Same as 1-4 of tripod technique.
     2. Insufficient lift of first leg and push with the second leg.

Figure 25

Tumbling and Acrobatic Skills

FORWARD ROLL (Fig. 26)

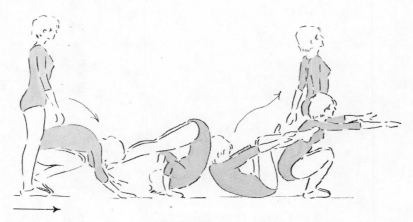

Figure 26

PT From a deep squat position with the knees together, place hands on mat approximately eighteen inches in front of the toes. Push down backward with the feet to extend legs and lift hips upward. Bend arms and lower upper shoulder area to mat (head tucks at the last possible second before shoulder contact). Keeping legs extended, continue rolling, and a soon as hips have contacted the mat, tuck the legs and come to a squat position reaching forward with the hands. Eyes spot stationary object after returning to a squat position to assist in maintaining balance and to help prevent dizziness when doing several in a row.

Hints: a. There should be a continuous motion from the squat position throughout the roll. If the performer stops or pauses in any one phase, it will be more difficult to complete the roll successfully.

b. The reason for keeping the legs extended while on the back in the inverted pike position and then forcefully tucking them as the hips contact the mat is to develop extra momentum to return to the squat position.

c. Having students learn to use their feet for pushing from the very beginning will enable them to catch onto other skills such as the dive roll more rapidly.

d. Have small youngsters or weak or overweight students roll down an inclined plane covered with a mat. This plane should be no more than a foot high. A reuther board or some homemade plank (both covered with a mat) could be used for this purpose.

SP   Kneel to side of performer. Place hand on back of head and neck to keep her from placing her head on the mat. If the performer has difficulty returning to a squat position after rolling, place hand on back and push to assist her in returning to the squat position.

CE   1. Incorrect hand placement on mat. Hands should not be placed to side of knees.
2. Failure to push with feet to develop momentum.
3. Failure to bend arms, tuck head, and place shoulders on the mat.
4. Tucking head too soon (results in back flopping to mat).
5. Failure to keep legs extended while rolling and then to tuck them forcefully as hips contact mat.
6. Placing hands on mat to assist body to squat position after rolling.

MO   1. Continuous forward rolls.
2. Forward rolls to single leg squat and pose.
3. Forward roll to knee and pose.
4. Forward roll to V sit.
5. Forward roll straddle to split.

VA   1. *Remain in tuck position throughout* (Fig. 27)

Figure 27

2. *From stand to single leg squat* (Fig. 28)

Figure 28

3. Forward roll to knee pose. (Fig. 29)

Figure 29

4. From stand to knee to splits. (Fig. 30)

Figure 30

5. From stoop position to stand. (Fig. 31)

Figure 31

6. *From straddle stand to straddle stand* (Fig. 32). As hips contact floor, place hands between legs (as close to body as possible) with fingers pointing forward to assist in pushing to straddle stand.

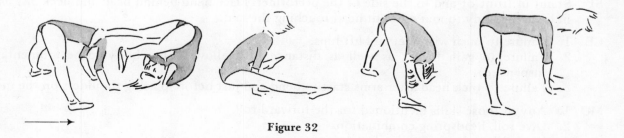

Figure 32

7. *Without hands* (Fig. 33). From deep lunge position tuck head and roll onto upper back and shoulder area allowing back of hand and arm to contact mat (out to side of body). End in any of above variations.

Figure 33

DIVE ROLL (Fig. 34)

1   2   3   4   5   6

Figure 34

PT Assume semi-squat position with shoulders forward of the feet and arms obliquely backward. Force arms forward and upward while simultaneously pushing with feet to extend legs and lift hips, causing the body to leave the mat and be suspended in air above the mat momentarily. Place hands on mat and *support* body weight. Bend arms with control, tuck head and lower upper shoulder area to mat and continue rolling.

Hints: a. Start from a deep squat position and gradually raise the body as confidence is gained. Eventually the skill should be executed from a standing position.
b. On all rolls forward, it is essential to keep the head up until the last possible second. However, if this is mentioned in the beginning phases of learning, some students tend to collapse and fall on their heads, especially those with weak arms. If your class is fairly strong, I would recommend emphasizing this point from the beginning.

SP Stand in front of and to the side of the performer. Place hand behind head and neck and assist in lowering body to mat without head touching the mat.

CE 1. Failure to push with feet and lift hips.
2. Failure to gain height as well as distance (not allowing the body to be momentarily suspended).
3. Failure to tuck head after arms start to bend and just before placing shoulders on the mat.

MO 1. Any of those skills mentioned for the forward roll.
2. Dive roll, headspring combination.
3. Dive roll, spring immediately into some type of jump.

VA 1. Dive over people or rolled up mats.
2. Dive through legs of person doing headstand with legs in straddle position.
3. Continuous dive rolls.
4. Dive through hula hoops.
5. Layout dive roll.

HANDSTAND

A good handstand position is a very important skill to master because the body passes through this position in performing many skills. It is advisable to learn where the body is and how or what it feels like partially upside down before attempting the handstand balanced position. One lead-up to the handstand should be a kick-up to near handstand position, switch legs and come to a stand.

Handstand kick-up (Fig. 35)

Figure 35

PT Lift arms overhead while simultaneously lifting left leg. Step forward onto left foot (as if making a small lunge) and bend left knee. Place hands on mat in front of shoulders. Swing right leg (straight) backward and upward. Immediately follow with a strong push from foot of left leg. Eyes spot hands. As soon as the body is almost inverted, switch legs and come to a stand on the right foot.

SP 1. Grasp above knee with both hands on one leg, stretch body to fullest.
2. Stand to side and forward of performer. Place inside arm across abdomen (palm up) grasping waist and outside hand (palm up) under shoulder to keep performer from collapsing.

CE 1. Failure to maintain straight arms.
2. Allowing shoulders to move forward of the hand position.
3. Not keeping the head in line with body.
4. Keeping the head too high.
5. Placing hands too far away or too close to the feet.
6. Insufficient kick, push, or both.

Balanced handstand (Fig. 36)

PT Use first five steps above for handstand switch legs. Maintain swing leg in air and bring push leg to meet it in the inverted position. Feel as if the entire body is pushing through the hands to make the toes reach the ceiling (by tightening muscles). The shoulders and hips should be extended.

Shoulders should be completely extended   **Figure 36**

CHECK POINTS FOR BALANCE
Shoulders over hands.
Hips over shoulders.
Heels over head.
Head in line with shoulders.

Hint: Use fingers (spread apart) to assist in balance by flexing them to feel as if they are trying to grasp the mat.

SP Stand to side (but forward of) performer. Grasp the leg (swing leg) above the knee as it reaches the inverted position. After student can almost balance herself, place arm (extended) toward back of her legs in case she should overbalance.

CE 1. Same as 1-5 in handstand kickup.
   2. Failure to extend shoulders and hips (body should be straight with slight arch in back).
   3. Allowing back to sag (body overarched).

MO 1. *Handstand forward roll* (Fig. 37)

Figure 37

PT Slightly overbalance, bend arms slowly; flex hips and go into pike position. Tuck head and place shoulders on mat and continue to roll.

CE Beginners have a tendency to keep arms straight too long, or tuck head too soon.

VA 1. Handstand forward roll with straight arms to pike.
   2. *Handstand pirouette (quarter or half turn) into limbre or walkover* (Fig. 38)

Figure 38

PT Shift weight to the hand that is in the direction of the turn. Quickly make turn, with eyes looking in the direction of the turn. Push off with, then lift opposite hand. After completing turn, go into limbre or walkover. Keep hips over shoulders throughout handstand position.

3. *Handstand snap down (Mule kick)* (Fig. 39)

Figure 39

PT Allow hips to lead body downward; flex knees slightly. Push forcefully from hands and lift chest while simultaneously thrusting from bent leg to extended leg position and land on mat.

CE Most common errors are not pushing with the hands and not coordinating the hand push, leg thrust and slight hip flexion.

4. *Handstand snap down back handspring step out* (Fig. 40). Refer to handstand snap down and then to back handspring step out.

Figure 40

5. *Handstand to splits* (Fig. 41)

PT Slightly overbalance handstand position. As body is beginning the downward movement, split the legs and force the leading leg downward and through arms as the shoulders extend, hands push from mat, and hips are raised. Finish in deep split position.

Figure 41

CE Most common error is not keeping the hips overhead when the leading leg begins a downward movement. When this occurs, there is not enough room to maintain straight leg position through the arms.

6. *Handstand chest roll* (Fig. 42)

PT While in handstand position, force head up and back as far as possible and maintain a very arched position. As the arms bend, lower the body to the mat, chest first, then roll until the toes contact the mat. Keep elbows close to the body when lowering the body to the mat. Finish in knee pose or roll on floor.

Figure 42

Figure 43

VA *Yogi handstand* (Fig. 43)

PT From handstand balanced position, flex the hips forcefully and allow legs to move into forward piked position. Simultaneously extend shoulders and bring head between arms to look at knees.

BACKWARD ROLL (Fig. 44)

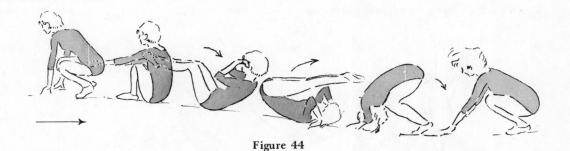

Figure 44

PT Assume a deep squat position with knees together (hands in front of body on mat partially supporting weight). Tuck head (chin on chest), push body backward off fingertips, and immediately transfer hands (palms up) to side of neck at shoulders. As hips contact mat, push downward on mat with feet and extend legs. Maintain straight legs until hands have contacted mat (palms down fingertips toward hips). Place toes on mat overhead and simultaneously tuck legs. As hips go overhead, keep elbows close to head and neck area, extend arms (push with hands) and come to squat position. Lift head.

SP Kneel to side of performer; as hips are brought to overhead position, grasp waist of performer and assist in lifting hips overhead to squat position.

CE 1. Not keeping back rounded on roll.
2. Incorrect placement of hands at shoulders. (Fingertips should point toward hips).
3. Failure to push with hands (extend arms) as hips pass overhead.
4. Pushing with one hand more than the other (results in a crooked roll).
5. Allowing the head to turn to the side.
6. Allowing knees to contact the mat instead of the toes.
7. Failure to eye spot when reaching squat position to assist in balance and prevent dizziness.

MO 1. Back roll to standing position.
2. Back roll to squat, then execute some type of jump.
3. Continuous backward rolls.
4. Back roll, backroll extension.

VA 1. *Back roll to knee scale* (Fig. 45)

Figure 45

2. *Back roll to straddle stand* (Fig. 46)

Figure 46

3. *Back roll from straddle position to end in straddle position* (Fig. 47)

Figure 47

4. *Back roll from stoop position* (Fig. 48). Shift hips backward, allowing shoulders to come forward. Keep arms straight and extended downbackward and upward as if to reach for mat. Slowly lose balance, keeping legs straight, causing body to go into deep pike position. Place hands on mat and immediately lower buttocks to mat and continue to roll.

Figure 48

BACK SHOULDER ROLL—over right shoulder (Fig. 49)

Figure 49

PT From a squat or sitting position, lower back to floor and lift legs upward straight and together. Have arms at side of body on the floor. Continue moving legs over body until toes touch floor over right shoulder. Head should be turned with eyes looking toward knees. At this point bend knees; keep looking at knees; left arm will come off the floor. Then transfer remainder of the body weight onto knees in a sitting position.

CE 1. Stopping in the middle of the skill, thus losing momentum needed to get hips over shoulder.
2. Not placing knees on floor close to shoulders.

MO 1. Toe rise.
2. Knee spin.
3. Forward roll.

BACK ROLL EXTENSION (Fig. 50)

Figure 50

PT Go through backward roll procedures to placing hands on mat under shoulders. As hips begin to pass over chest, thrust the legs by extending upward while simultaneously pushing with the hands (extend arms) against the mat. Lift head, arch back, and come to a momentary handstand position. Snap down to standing position or lower one leg at a time.

Hint: Have spotter assist in performing this skill slowly, so the performer will know at what point in the roll to extend and what extending the arms in an inverted position feels like.

SP Stand to the side and in front of the performer. As the legs begin to thrust vertically, grasp the legs above the knee and assist in lifting body to handstand position.

CE 1. Thrusting the legs too soon or too late.
2. Failure to thrust the legs vertically and push with the hands simultaneously.
3. Insufficient thrust of legs, insufficient push with hands, or both.
4. Failure to lift up back and arch back when arms extend.
5. Failure to attain handstand position before returning to mat.

MO 1. Snap down, back handspring.
2. Back extension, back roll.
3. Back extension to split (covered in handstand variations).
4. Back extension straddle down (covered in handstand variations).
5. Back extension stoop through.

VA *Back roll extension step out* (Fig. 51)

Figure 51

PT Performed the same as the back roll extension except, when the body reaches the handstand position, one leg is lowered to the mat before the other.

SP Same as the back roll extension.

CARTWHEEL (left) (Fig. 53)

Figure 52. Cartwheel

Figure 53. Cartwheel quarter turn

PT   Facing forward, lift arms overhead while lifting left leg. Step forward onto left foot (bend knee) while shifting weight to that foot. Place left hand on mat with fingers pointing to left side of body (hand placement is to be directly in front of the body). Forcefully swing the right leg upward and immediately follow with a strong push from the foot of the left leg. (The legs maintain a straddle position throughout entire skill.) As the body executes 90° turn, the right hand is placed on the mat about fourteen to eighteen inches directly in front of (and forward of) left hand. Push off the mat (about twenty inches or more from left hand) with slightly bent knee. As the left foot contacts the mat, the right leg is already in motion with a backupward swing. Right leg extends and the upper body is raised. The entire body ends up facing 90° (quarter turn) right of starting position. The eyes spot the hands as they are placed on the mat.

Hint: This is a four count skill: hand, hand, foot, foot.

SP   For left cartwheel: Just the opposite for right. Stand to left side and back of performer. Cross arms, right under left. As performer places hands on mat, cross hands and grasp waist. Assist throughout movement. Hands will uncross and cross again in the process. If the performer has difficulty with the second leg (left), slide the right hand to thigh and force the leg upward.

CE   1. Placing hands on mat simultaneously.
      2. Placing the hands to the left of the body rather than directly forward in front of body.
      3. Placing left hand too close or too far from left foot.
      4. Insufficient swing from right leg, insufficient push from left foot, or both.
      5. Allowing shoulders and upper body to turn before hands are placed on the mat. This skill should be done in a straight line.
      6. Allowing legs to close while inverted.
      7. Failure to maintain straight arms and legs.
      8. Allowing right foot to contact mat before left hand leaves.
      9. Allowing hip to flex while inverted.
   10. Failure to eye spot hands as they are placed on the mat.
   11. Failure to land with right leg slightly bent and to raise the body as the right leg is extending.
   12. Failure to keep arms by head throughout skill.

MO   1. Quarter turn and a second cartwheel.
      2. Quarter turn and stop in a handstand.
      3. Quarter turn to any locomotor skill.
      4. Quarter turn and cartwheel to opposite side.

VA 1. *One-handed cartwheel near arm* (Fig. 54a)

Figure 54a

2. *One-handed cartwheel far arm* (Fig. 54b)

Figure 54b

3. *Dive cartwheel* (Fig. 55). Usually preceded by a hurdle. Same preparation as for cartwheel. Begin kicking and very strong pushing action, lifting the head and chest; reach forward and upward before placing the hands on mat. There will be a stronger push from the hands, and they will contact the mat almost simultaneously.

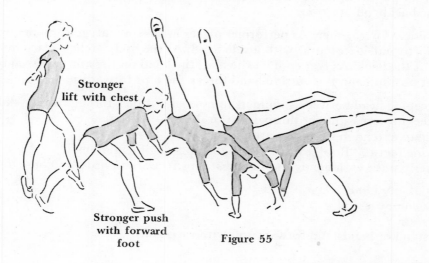

Stronger lift with chest

Stronger push with forward foot

Figure 55

LIMBRE (Fig. 56)

Figure 56

PT Kick to momentary handstand with eyes looking at fingers. Extend shoulders behind hand placement. As balance is lost, legs will move in an arc; arch back and *place* feet on mat so that body is in momentary backbend position. As soon as feet are flat on mat, push with hands and force hips forward over feet to allow the legs to extend (straighten knees). Arms are kept up by head until standing position is achieved.

Hint: Head position is very important. The head, along with the arms, must be kept back at all times. If the head and arms are brought forward, the body will collapse into a sitting position. It is also very important to fully extend shoulders to cause the body to overbalance in order to go into the backbend position.

SP Stand to side of performer. As performer places hands on mat, grasp upper arm (with palm up and thumb to outside of arm) with inside hand. As the body arches, place the outside hand on the small of the back. As feet contact the mat, the hand on the arm assists in bringing the body to an erect position and the outside hand forces the hips forward so legs can extend.

CE 1. Not keeping head between shoulders in normal position through entire skill.
2. Not keeping arms straight through entire skill.
3. Failure to extend in shoulders after inverting.
4. Allowing feet to "flop" to mat rather than placing them on mat.
5. Failure to push with hands and to thrust hips forward in order to come to stand.

MO 1. Turns of any kind.
2. Any locomotor skill.
3. Walkover.
4. Handstand or handstand forward roll with variations.

FRONT WALKOVER (Fig. 57)

Figure 57

PT Lift arms over head while simultaneously lifting left leg. Step forward onto left foot (small lunge) shifting weight to left foot. Place hands on mat, shoulder width apart, and immediately swing right leg upward to invert the body. Immediately push with the left foot (extend leg). Extend in the shoulders so that they go behind the heel of the hands. Keeping the legs in a wide stride position, allow the back to arch and *place* the right foot on the mat (close to the midline of the body). Push with hands and thrust hips forward and straighten right knee. Come to an erect position on the right foot keeping head, arms and shoulders back until a controlled erect position is achieved. Left leg should be kept up high so it can be placed down on mat. Keep left foot extended in front.

Hint: Think of stepping over a hurdle with the left foot in order to keep it extended until the erect position has been achieved.

SP Same as for limbre.

CE 1. Not keeping arms straight throughout.
2. Not keeping arms by head throughout.
3. Failure to extend shoulders behind the hands.
4. Not arching lower back.
5. Failure to *place* foot on mat.
6. Allowing legs to go over crooked (to side of body rather than in vertical plane).
7. Not pushing with hands and thrusting hips forward.
8. Allowing second leg to catch up to first leg and be placed on the mat.

MO 1. Any locomotor skill.
2. Continuous walkovers.
3. Handstand.

VA 1. *Switch legs while inverted*
(Fig. 58)

Figure 58

2. *Scissors leg while inverted* (Fig. 59)

Figure 59

BACK WALKOVER (Fig. 60)

Figure 60

PT Stand on left foot with the toes of right foot on the mat and about eight to fourteen inches in front of the left. Lift arms foreupward, stretch (extend) vertically in the shoulders, tilt the head back (between arms), and allow the back to arch. (Keep hips over left foot until last possible moment. This will stretch the shoulders more.) As the hands contact the mat (about shoulder width apart), the right leg lifts vigorously upward and overhead. The left foot immediately pushes off the mat to allow the body to be inverted with legs in a wide stride (split) position. As the right foot contacts the mat with a slight knee bend, the hands push off the mat, and the body is raised to an erect position with left leg extended to the rear. After skill is learned, start with forward leg parallel to floor or higher.

SP Stand to side of performer. Place inside hand on lower back and outside hand on back of upper thigh of front leg. Assist by supporting lower back, and help lift forward leg as hands contact mat.

CE 1. Failure to start with weight on one foot.
2. Failure to extend shoulders as well as to arch the back.
3. Allowing the hips to move forward of the feet while going into backbend position.
4. Not maintaining straight arms.
5. Not lifting forward leg vigorously as hands contact mat.
6. Failure to push off with hands and lift upper body as first foot contacts mat.
7. Failure to keep legs in a wide stride position.
8. Allowing legs to go out to side of body rather than moving in a vertical plane.

MO 1. Any locomotor skill.
    2. Consecutive back walkovers.
    3. Back walkover, back handspring. Bring second leg to mat beside first foot and immediately spring into back handspring.

VA 1. *Back walkover to splits.* From inverted position with legs in wide stride position, slightly overbalance and extend shoulders. Lift chest and forcefully thrust lead leg (leg in rear) between arms. Refer to figure 41.
    2. *Back walkover to handstand straddle down* (Fig. 61). Gain balance in handstand position from walkover. Allow shoulders to move slightly forward of the hand position as the legs move to a wide straddle position. Flex hips and allow shoulders to move backward of hand position. Lower hips to floor with legs in wide straddle position.

Figure 61

KIP (Fig. 62)

PT From supine position on mat, lift legs and flex hips (together and straight) overhead, touching toes on mat behind head. Place hands under shoulders with fingertips pointing toward hips. Lower hips slightly; then simultaneously thrust legs forward, upward, and outward, and push forcefully with hands. Keeping arms straight and head up and back, come to stand with body fully extended (slight knee bend to absorb shock).

Figure 62

Hint: Learn to thrust legs first by extending hips vigorously. Then practice thrusting legs and pushing with arms to get into backbend (bridge) position.

SP Kneel (one knee) to side of performer. Place inside hand on upper arm and outside hand on small of back as leg thrust begins.

CE 1. Failure to lower hips before thrusting legs and pushing with hands.
    2. Insufficient thrust with legs, insufficient push with hands, or both.
    3. Leg thrust and hand push not simultaneous.
    4. Failure to keep head up and back until standing.
    5. Failure to keep arms back overhead until standing.

HEADSPRING (Fig. 63)

Figure 63

PT   From squat position, place head and hands on mat forming a triangle. Place toes on mat with slight knee bend. Push through toes, extending legs and forcing hips to an overhead position. Keep the body in a pike position; as the hips continue past head position and loss of balance occurs, force (heels first) the legs foreupward (extending hips) and simultaneously push forcefully with the hands. Body is fully extended with arms over head as feet contact mat (with slight knee bend).

Hint: Sometimes it is advantageous to learn this on a rolled up mat.

SP   Kneel (on one knee) beside performer. Inside hand grasps upper arm and outside hand supports lower back.

CE   1.   Failure to allow hips to pass head position before thrusting legs and pushing with hands.
     2.   Failure to keep in tight pike as hips are going to overhead position.
     3.   Same as 2-5 in the kip.

MO   1.   Any locomotor skill.
      2.   Another tumbling skill such as dive roll.

VALDEZ (Fig. 64)

Leg should be
straight here

Figure 64

PT   Sit on floor with left knee to chest (foot flat on floor), right leg extended. Put left hand on floor behind hips with arm straight and right arm forward horizontal. Thrust the right arm overhead while simultaneously extending the left leg and kicking with the right leg to push the body to an inverted position. As the body is reaching the inverted position, place the right hand on the floor next to the left (shoulder width apart) and rotate the left hand around so that both hands are pointing forward. Lower one leg at a time as in a back walkover.

SP   Kneel at left side and place inside hand on lower back and outside hand on back of upper thigh. Assist in lifting to inverted position.

CE   1.   Insufficient kick, push, or both.
     2.   Allowing arms to bend.
     3.   Not thrusting hips upward with leg push.

VA Some people prefer to have the forward arm on the same side as the bent leg.

HURDLE (Fig. 65)

European hurdle   American hurdle

Figure 65

A hurdle is a step hop preceded by 1 or 2 running steps. It is used to transfer forward momentum up, then forward again with added force from the take-off foot (push leg).

To practice: Step right, step left, hop left while keeping right leg behind and lifting arms overhead. Step onto right foot (bent leg) and immediately push from mat (extend leg) and lift the body vertically. Left leg is now behind and ready to kick backupward.

When coordination is learned, add 1 or 2 running steps. Allow each student to use the side that feels most comfortable to her for performing the hurdle.

FRONT HANDSPRING (Fig. 66)

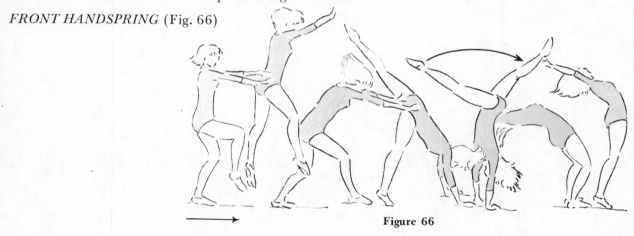

Figure 66

Note: Basic tumbling skills such as front handspring, round-off, round-off back handspring should be learned from a step without a hurdle. This forces the student to make maximum use of explosive leg power.

PT Execute hurdle. Step onto right foot, bending knee. Place hands on mat in front of right foot (about eighteen inches) while simultaneously swinging left leg backupward. Immediately execute a very strong push with the right leg (which is bent under body) so that the legs will meet as the body passes through the handstand position. Extend shoulders backward, arch back, and as balance is lost (when the legs and hips pass over hands), push the body away from the mat with the hands and shoulders. The body is momentarily suspended in air in a fully extended position (arched). Reach for the mat with the toes. Body should be slightly arched upon landing, with head back, arms overhead, and a slight knee bend.

Hint: On the front handspring, front handspring step out, and tinsica, the legs are mainly responsible for inverting and rotating the body. The kick-push action of the legs should be emphasized along with the fact that, if the pushing action starts slightly before the hands contact the mat, the body will invert faster. If the kick-push action is quick and strong, the hands will support the entire body weight for a very short duration. Also, overbalancing from the inverted position can occur much faster so that the arms and hands do not push "dead weight."

SP Same as for front limbre.

CE 1. Uncoordinated hurdle and step.
    2. Placing hands on mat before initial kick is made.
    3. Placing the hands too close or too far away from the feet.
    4. Insufficient thrust of right leg (extended leg); insufficient push from left bent leg.
    5. Failure to extend shoulders, keep body stretched, and maintain arms overhead until feet make contact with the mat (knees slightly bent to absorb shock and assist in maintaining balance).

Note: When head and arms come forward after the hands leave the mat, this usually causes the hips to flex and the body to fall backward or finish the skill in a squat position.

MO 1. Step into any locomotor skill.
    2. Front handspring, handstand forward roll.
    3. Front handspring, walkover.
    4. Front handspring, squat jump, back roll extension.
    5. Front handspring to straddle seat.

VA 1. *Front handspring step out* (Fig. 67)

Notice total body lift

Figure 67

   PT Execute on the same principles of the handspring, but keep legs in a wide stride position throughout (as in a walkover). There must be a very strong kick and push with the foot of the second leg and with the hands so that the body will return to the mat with the lead leg almost straight and the hips forward of the foot that contacts the mat first. Keep head up and back at all times.

   CE 1. Same as 1-5 in handspring.
       2. Failure to keep legs in a wide stride position throughout.
       3. Failure to land on lead foot with hips forward of that foot.

MO 1. Any locomotor skill.
      2. Consecutive handspring step outs.
      3. Round-off.
      4. Aerial cartwheel or aerial walkover (front and side aerials).

2. *Front handspring step out switching legs* (Fig. 68)

Hips should be more forward over left foot.

Figure 68

PT Use same principles as for the handspring step out except that, while in the inverted position, reverse leg positions so that the back leg becomes the forward leg.

CE Most common error is switching legs too soon or too late or allowing the (either) leg to be directed sideways rather than straight forward.

SP Same as for front handspring.

3. *Front handspring to straddle seat* (Fig. 69)

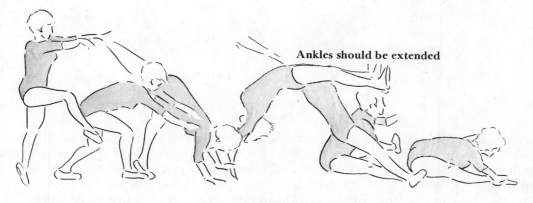

Ankles should be extended

Figure 69

FRONT HANDSPRING FRONT SOMMIE (Fig. 70)

Figure 70

PT From a well-executed front handspring, "punch" the mat with the feet, keeping arms in the vertical position. Spring *upward*; then whip the arms down and tuck head to chest, as hips flex and knees bend to chest. Rotate three-quarters of a full spin; then extend legs, hips, and upper body to a stand.

SP As soon as the feet are ready to land from the front handspring, place the near arm (hand) across the abdomen with the palm up. As the performer is springing vertically, lift far arm upward to grasp her back and rotate body.

CE 1. Stopping after front handspring.
2. Tucking head and lowering arms before vertical lift.
3. Poor "punch" from mat, creating inadequate vertical lift.
4. Opening tuck too soon or to late.

Note: Whenever two skills are put together e.g., front handspring front, round-off back handspring, etc., performer must execute first skill well and anticipate landing so explosive punch can occur for second skill.

MO 1. Round-off back handspring.
2. Forward roll back handspring.
3. Any kind of dance turn.

VA Front handspring, front sommie with a step-out (front handspring front aerial step-out).

TINSICA (Fig. 71)

Figure 71

PT Execute this skill as if you were going to do a handspring step out. The major difference is the hand placement on the mat. After the hurdle, step onto the right foot, bending the knee; simultaneously swing left leg upward, and immediately start the pushing action of the right foot. Place the right hand on the mat about eighteen inches in front of the right foot, and then place the left hand in front of the right hand (approximately ten to sixteen inches). Eyes spot hands as they are placed on the mat. The head remains up and back throughout the skill. As the body overbalances (hips falling toward mat), vigorously push with the hands and extend the shoulders. Maintain the legs in a stride position and land on the left foot, push the hips forward, and immediately step into the right foot (Fig. 71).

SP Same as for front handspring.

CE In general, they are the same as for the handspring step out, plus failure to place the hands on the mat one after the other (in a straight line) and failure to allow the second foot to contact the mat after the first foot makes contact.

MO 1. Into any locomotor skill.
2. Consecutive tinsicas.
3. Tinsica, dive cartwheel.
4. Tinsica into round-off.

ROUND-OFF (Fig. 72)

Legs should be together in vertical position

Punch and vertical lift

Figure 72

The primary purpose of the round-off is to change forward momentum into rearward movement.

PT From a hurdle, step onto right foot, bending knee. Swing left foot forcefully backupward, and begin pushing action with the right foot as the right hand contacts the mat in a direct line of the body, with the fingers pointing to the right side of the body. Immediately place the left hand on the mat (about five inches in front of the right) with fingers facing to the right of the body. As the body passes through a handstand position, it will complete a 180° (half) turn. Force legs together while inverted (before the turn), and as the body is overbalanced, push hard with the hands and shoulders. Flex hips, force feet close to hand placement, lift the upper body. As feet contact mat immediately punch and lift vertical.

Hint: Go through the skill in slow motion without a hurdle to get the feeling of bringing the legs together and turning before snapping the legs down. Have students jump (spring up) immediately upon landing as if rebounding. This forces them to push with their hands and raise their heads and chests as their feet snap to the mat.

SP When going through the skill in slow motion, spot as if spotting for a cartwheel. When performing from a hurdle, stand to the nonturning side and grasp hip area.

CE 1. Not placing hands on mat in direct line with body.
2. Insufficient kick, push, or both.
3. Failure to bring legs together and pass through vertical before completing the half (180°) turn.
4. Failure to push with the hands and lift the head and chest after feet have passed handstand position.
5. Failure to keep legs straight and together (slight knee bend when landing).
6. Failure to rebound vertically upon landing.

MO 1. Back roll extension.
2. Back handspring.
3. Back handspring series.
4. Back handspring, back sommie.
5. Back sommie.
6. Back aerial layout.

BACK HANDSPRING (Fig. 73)

Figure 73

PT Stand with feet parallel and together. Keep arms at front of body and parallel to floor. Flex knees and hips keeping shoulders over hips and begin to move backward as if to sit in a chair. As the sitting movement begins, the arms move downbackward. When balance is lost push vigorously with the legs and simultaneously force the arms foreupward and overhead. Extend in shoulders, and reach for the mat with the hands. The body is suspended in air momentarily before the hands contact the mat (shoulder width apart and approximately three feet from foot placement on the mat). Just after the hands contact the mat and the body passes through a handstand position, flex the hips and force (snap) the legs and feet to the mat while simultaneously pushing from the mat with the hands and lifting the head and upper body. Keep head in normal body alignment to prevent undercutting.

SP Stand to side of performer. Place inside hand on back of upper thigh and outside hand on small of back. Use outside hand to assist performer to maintain an arched position and to keep her from falling on her head (if she should bend her arms). Inside hand assists with leg thrust and snap down to stand.

Hint: Some people find it helpful to start from a squat position, rock forward, then continue with above procedures from the squat position. Spotter on one knee with hands in same position as above.

CE 1. Failure to maintain shoulders over hips when sitting backward to lose balance.
2. Insufficient thrust of arms backward.
3. Allowing arms to bend when hands contact the mat.
4. Failure to keep legs together after takeoff.
5. Pushing with the feet too soon or too late.
6. Insufficient push with the feet and picking feet up from mat instead of allowing upper body to pull legs over.
7. Flexing hips too soon or too late (not allowing the body to pass through a handstand position).
8. Not extending the shoulders, pushing away from the mat with the hands, and not lifting the head and chest as the feet are about to contact the mat.
9. Allowing the feet to flop to the mat rather than being forced down.

MO 1. Continuous back handsprings.
2. Back flip.
3. Back aerial layout.
4. Jump, then to any other locomotor skill.
5. Split.

VA *Back handspring step out* (Fig. 74)

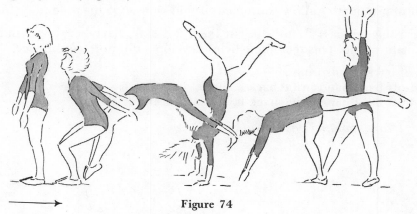

Figure 74

PT Same beginning procedure as for the back handspring. As the body is passing through the handstand position, allow the body to slightly overarch, maintain one leg inverted, allow the other foot to be placed on the mat. Place the second foot on the mat. Foot placement on the mat is the same as for back walkover.

SP Same as for back handspring.

ROUND-OFF BACK HANDSPRING (Fig. 75)

Figure 75

PT It is one thing to do the back handspring alone and the round-off as a single skill, but it is difficult to get a student to do them together for the first time. Some fear is involved as a change of direction is required while upside down. Go through the first couple in slow motion, but do not attempt to put the skills together until both are learned well. As the feet are coming down in the round-off, they should drive toward the hands. (This is to get the body into position so that it can go immediately backward). As the feet contact the mat the knees are slightly bent with head and chest forward. The arms and upper body immediately extend upward and backward, and the legs extend explosively to complete the back handspring.

CE 1. Inadequate leg thrust on the round-off causing loss of momentum.
2. Not driving the legs under the body enough in the round-off.
3. Stopping between the two skills.

SP Have a designated spot for the performer to start and for her to place her hands on the round-off. Stand about two feet beyond hand placement area. As soon as the performer is coming down out of the round-off, place your outside hand on small of back and inside hand on back of upper thigh. Follow through as if you were spotting a standing back handspring.

Hint: In the learning process if the student fears this skill, have her do a handstand, snap down, then back handspring. This technique helps develop a bit more confidence.

MO 1. Series of back handsprings.
2. Round-off back handspring back sommie.
3. Round-off back handspring back layout or full twist.

BACK SOMMIE (from standing position) (Fig. 76)

Poor body position. Lift should be vertical rather than backward.

Figure 76

PT Bend knees slightly and spring vertically, swinging the arms vigorously foreupward to assist in gaining height. As maximum height is attained, drive the knees to the chest, and rotate rearward in a tuck position. As eyes contact spotting point, extend the legs, keep raising upper body, and land on mat with with knees slightly bent. Keep head between shoulders throughout.

Note: Before performer begins back sommie, she should pick out an object at eye level to keep looking for during rotation.

SP 1. Use spotting belt.
2. One spotter to each side of the performer. Place inside hand on small of back (grasp garment if necessary) and lift or support throughout the skill. The outside hand is placed on the back of the thigh as soon as possible after tuck position is attained and assists in rotating the body. Never lose contact with the performer.

CE 1. Throwing head back any time during skill
2. Failure to spring vertically.
3. Failure to gain sufficient height on jump.
4. Failure to force knees to chest and stay in tight tuck until ready to open.
5. Opening tuck position to soon or too late.

VA 1. *Round-off back sommie* (Fig. 77)

Figure 77

PT When performing the back sommie or back layout out of a round-off, the feet do not drive in toward the hands as much as they do for the back handspring because on the sommie or layout the entire body must go directly upward before rotating. As the feet contact the mat from the round-off, the arms lift vertically as if jumping to reach the ceiling, with the head in normal position. *The feet in essence "punch" the mat so the lift can be rapid and high.* When reaching the peak of the lift, the knees thrust toward the chest, the head is in normal position, and the body starts rotation. When three-fourths of the sommie has been completed, extend hips and legs and lift upper body and head.

SP Same as for round-off back handspring. Make sure contact is made on the round-off.

CE 1. Stopping after the round-off—move must be continuous.
2. Not punching the mat out of the round-off to make the vertical lift.
3. Throwing the head and arms BACK immediately out of the round-off.
4. Not tucking enough.
5. Opening tuck position too soon or too late.

2. *Round-off back handspring, back flip*

ROUND-OFF BACK LAYOUT (Fig. 78)

Figure 78

PT From the round-off or round-off back handspring, "punch" the mat with the feet and immediately spring upward while lifting arms overhead. Squeeze the hips as tight as possible and *lift with the chest.* When maximum height is almost reached, tilt head slightly backward and *keep lifting chest and squeezing hips.* If body is kept completely tight, it will rotate around the head position. At this point arms may be kept at the side of the body.

Hint: Learn layout on trampoline first.

Tumbling and Acrobatic Skills   **41**

SP As soon as performer lands from the round-off or back handspring, place hands on small of back and hip area. If the individual has learned this skill well enough on the trampoline first, all the spotter should have to do is assist with the lift.

CE 1. Throwing head and arms back immediately—should go UP.
2. Failure to lift with chest.
3. Failure to keep hips and legs tight and together.

VA Layout step-out.
When body is inverted in layout position, split legs and keep them split; then land on one foot followed by the other in a lunge position.

FULL TWIST (Fig. 79)

Figure 79

PT (Must learn good back layout first. Learn the twist on the trampoline first.) From a back handspring or round-off, "punch" the mat and lift vertically as if to do a back layout. As the body starts backward motion, turn the head over left shoulder and look for the left hip area. Left arm can rest on chest at this point and right remains up. Keep looking for the hip and, as the body rotates, pull right arm across chest and left arm lifts up. As one-half of the spin is completed, both arms will be in front of the body, usually crossed. Eyes focus on the mat at this time and remain focused here until the skill is completed. As the feet pass the head position, the hips will slightly flex before landing. Both hands will lift to forward-upward position. Body must stay tight throughout the entire skill.

SP Learn on trampoline using twisting belt.
Use twisting belt on floor until adjusted to twisting on mats.

CARTWHEEL AERIAL (to the left) (Fig. 80a)

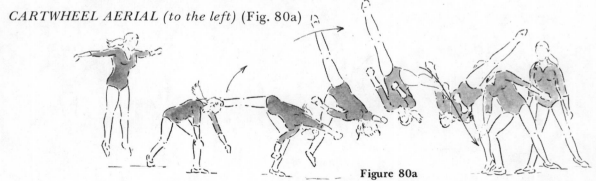

Figure 80a

PT From hurdle, step forward, *keeping the head and chest high and not allowing the chest to go forward of the foot position* and forcefully swing the right leg backupward; then immediately push very strongly with the left foot. Put arms up on the hurdle, and as the swing-push leg action is started, swing them down to the side of the body. The arms may keep moving with the body or may be brought to the side of the body and bend and remain in this position throughout. As the right foot lands on the mat, followed by the left foot, lift the head and chest.

Lead-ups:
1. Cartwheel from lunge to lunge inward.
2. Dive cartwheel, then dive cartwheel with one hand.
3. Use reuther board to get extra spring.

SP 1. Place inside hand palm up on abdomen. Place outside hand on shoulder with fingers pointed toward floor. As performer rotates, support body with hand on shoulder and lift waist area forcefully up and over with hand that is on waist area.
2. Stand to nonturning side of body; place both hands in hip and thigh area and lift (Fig. 80b).

Figure 80b

3. Stand to nonturning side of the performer. As the body is turning to inverted position, grasp waist and assist by lifting the entire body as with regular cartwheel (Fig. 80c).

Figure 80c

CE 1. Uncoordinated hurdle.
2. Allowing the shoulders and head to drop too far forward or move forward of the feet.
3. Insufficient swing, push of the legs, or both.
4. Not allowing the body to make quarter (90°) turn as push foot leaves mat.
5. Failure to place leading foot under body as much as possible.
6. Failure to continue lifting head and chest upon landing.

Note: The body when finishing should be facing more the direction of the skill when started rather than directly sideways.

VA Glide aerial. (chassé aerial)

FRONT AERIAL (Fig. 81a)

Figure 81a

PT   From hurdle, lean slightly forward keeping head and chest high. *Do not allow shoulders to go forward of the feet. Vigorously* swing backupward with the back foot; then *immediately* push with the forward foot. Bring arms from overhead position to sides of the body or allow them to continue backward. Arch the back and maintain legs in a wide split position. Land on swing leg first. When foot contacts mat, keep head back and chest up.

Hint: Learn from standing position. One spotter to each side of the performer. Grasp hand and as performer is inverting, place other hand on shoulder to assist in lifting throughout skill.

SP   1.   Stand to side of performer. Place inside hand on abdomen as skill is started. Lift and support about halfway through. Put outside hand on small of back; lift and support through the last half of the skill (Fig. 81b).

Figure 81b

    2.   Stand to side of performer, and as shoulders move forward, place inside hand on abdomen and outside hand under shoulder and assist in lifting throughout rotation. This method is also used for side aerial.

CE   1.   Same as 1-3 in aerial cartwheel.

2. Failure to keep the legs in a wide split position throughout.
3. Failure to continue keeping chest and head up after landing on first foot.

Tumbling Routines for Class

Tumbling routines for class will depend on the ability level of the students involved. Each class should be given routines that they can perform with little difficulty but that will be challenging. Performers should start and end routines at attention or some other static position.

Suggested routines:
1. Forward roll, dive roll, forward roll coming up to squat position, execute jump with half (90°) turn, back roll.
2. Dive roll, forward roll, cartwheel with quarter turn, forward roll.
3. Back roll coming to squat position, execute jump with half turn, forward roll to stand, cartwheel with quarter turn, dive roll.
4. Handstand forward roll, dive roll, dive roll, round-off to vertical jump.
5. Dive roll to stand, limbre, limbre, front walkover.
6. Dive roll, headspring, dive roll, round-off, vertical jump, back roll extension.
7. Front handspring, cartwheel with quarter turn, limbre, walkover.
8. Back handspring, back walkover, half turn, cartwheel with quarter turn.
9. Round-off back handspring, back roll, back roll extension.
10. Round-off back handspring, back handspring step out.
11. Front handspring step out, round-off back handspring.

NOTES

CHAPTER THREE
FLOOR EXERCISE

Floor exercise is the most beautiful event in women's gymnastics. To perform well in this event, a gymnast must be an "actress on the floor," able to convey a feeling or create an atmosphere that will stimulate and impress the audience and judges.

In competition, the exercise is performed in a 12 x 12 meter area. The gymnast must cover the entire area within the sixty-to-ninety-second time limit.

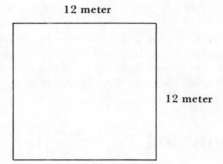

12 meter

12 meter

Components of a Floor Exercise Routine

1. *Tumbling and acrobatic skills* must be incorporated with smooth transitions into and out of moves.
2. *Dance.* Ballet, modern, and jazz dance skills are used mainly as connecting moves or as static and semi-static position. They are also used to vary the tempo and for change of direction.
3. *Locomotor skills.* Skills such as leaps, hops, and jumps add variety to a routine. They are used to vary the tempo and level and to give the routine a more dynamic and explosive appearance.
4. *Static positions.* Poses and holds are included in a routine for variations in tempo and level so that the routine will not be monotonous. Poses are held only long enough to show control in that particular position or to gain a desired effect; holds are held for three seconds.
5. *Variations in level.* A routine should be composed of skills on the floor (e.g., splits) and in the air (e.g., leaps) and positions that could be considered a middle level (e.g., arabesque).
6. *Changes in direction.* Changes should be fluid and varied (e.g., battement tourney, chainé turn, round-off, reversed stag leap).
7. *Variations in tempo.* A good routine is not monotonous since some of the movements included are fast, slow, percussive, sustained, etc. These movements or sequences should fit and express the tempo of the music used.
8. *Floor pattern.* A floor design that meets the requirement of covering the entire area and allows the gymnast to move with grace and continuity is of utmost importance. Skills should not always be performed in a straight line but should vary in different patterns that will add to the beauty of the routine.
9. *Dynamic opening and ending.* Whether slow or fast, the opening of a routine should set the stage for the remainder of the exercise. The ending should also be dynamic and should convey a happy feeling.

10. *Difficulty.* A competitive routine must contain six elements of difficulty, two superior difficulties and four medium. These can be tumbling, dance, or locomotor skills, or combinations of these skills. A list of these difficulties can be found in the F.I.G. code of points.

11. *Use of entire body.* The entire body must be used in a routine. Body lines are important for aesthetic beauty and can be varied to meet this requirement. Moves of flexibility and agility must be shown, but moves of strength must be avoided.

12. *Music.* The music, which must be played by a single instrument, should fit the routine. It must be dynamic when the skill combinations are dynamic, light when the skill combinations are light, etc.

Composition

A gymnast has almost unlimited freedom when composing a routine because she must conform only to the basic rules of time, difficulty, space to be covered, and form. Creating or putting together combinations of tumbling and acrobatic skills, ballet, modern dance, and jazz moves, and locomotor skills in an original and exciting manner is not an easy task. Most gymnasts change sequences in a routine many times before the entire routine is fluid, enlightening, and completely harmonious throughout.

If a girl is strong in tumbling, she should include many tumbling sequences, along with meeting the other requirements of composition. If a girl is proficient in dance, many dance combinations should be included as long as they do not dominate the routine.

Changes of direction and passes should not be repetitious; they should be fluid, elegant, and express the creative ability of the performer. *Be original.*

Dance for the Gymnast

One does not have to spend years training in ballet technique to become proficient and graceful in performing dance skills in the floor exercise event. It is always advantageous, though, to have some type of training or exposure to dance to learn proper body carriage and skill techniques.

The following skills have been selected for description since they are adaptable to movement in floor exercise or are excellent exercises to develop leg strength and proper body positions. The skills will be divided into two categories: (1) ballet and (2) modern and jazz.

BALLET

FUNDAMENTAL POSITIONS FOR THE ARMS AND FEET

In all positions you should be concerned with correct body alignment. Abdomen is taut, shoulders relaxed, and hips pulled under the body causing the back to be more straight than curved. Head should be up at all times.

FIRST POSITION (Fig. 82)

Arms: Held in a circular pattern in front of and away from the body. The elbows are slightly bent so that the hands are just below waist level. It is helpful to think that you are holding a very large ball. Palms face inward.

Feet: Heels are together with toes pointing outward. Force the little toe on to the floor to maintain correct arch in the foot.

Figure 82

SECOND POSITION (Fig. 83)

Arms: Held sideways with a very slight bend in the elbow to give a soft rather than a rigid appearance. Make sure that the arms are slightly forward of the body and the thumb is under the second finger (as if holding a small ball with the thumb and finger). Palms face down. First finger is the extension of the arm. It is now acceptable to have the palms face forward and upward depending on the move being performed.

Feet: In same position as for that of first position but about twelve inches apart.

Figure 83

FOURTH POSITION (Fig. 84)

Arms: One is in second position, the other in high fifth (which is curved overhead and slightly in front of the body).

Feet: One foot approximately twelve inches in front of the other with the heel of the forward foot in line with the arch of the back foot.

FIFTH POSITION (Fig. 85)

Arms: Both arms curved overhead and slightly in front of the head.

Feet: Heel of right foot against toe of left foot. Toe of right foot against heel of left foot. May be reversed with left in front.

Figure 84

Figure 85

Many girls look awkward, clumsy, or unpolished in floor exercise simply because they do not know what to do with their arms. Arms are very important in creating proper body lines. This part of the body should not be neglected when training for the floor exercise event.

The arms should hold a definite position and move smoothly from one skill to another, avoiding very jerky or wavering movements (unless for a specific effect). Always think of the arms as coming from the middle of the back rather than from the shoulder joint.

EXERCISES FOR DEVELOPING PROPER FLEXIBILITY AND BODY POSITIONS FOR DANCE MOVES

DEMI PLIÉ (This may be done in any position) (Fig. 86)

PT Keeping upper body erect, bend the knees and return to original position. Heels must remain in constant contact with the floor.

Note: Pliés are very important for developing flexibility in the legs and for upper body control. They are used when taking off and landing in locomotor, tumbling, and dance skills. Pliés should be done daily as a part of conditioning. It is suggested that they be done in all positions, both at a barre and away from a barre. If a barre is not available, a chair will suffice.

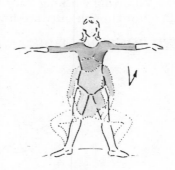

Figure 86

CE 1. Allowing shoulders to move forward of the hips.
2. Allowing back to curve greatly with the hips protruding in the rear rather than keeping them under the shoulders.
3. Allowing the heels to come off of the floor.
4. Allowing the knees to stay to the medial line of the body rather than come outward directly in line with the toes.

BATTEMENT TENDU (Fig. 87)

PT Starting position: Arms in second, feet in fifth. Lift the heel of the forward foot and slide the foot as far out as possible. Place the heel down and snap back to fifth position with the heel leading.

CE 1. Poor body alignment.
2. Allowing back leg to bend.
3. Allowing supporting hip to relax (sag).
4. Allowing forward leg to bend when returning to the original position.

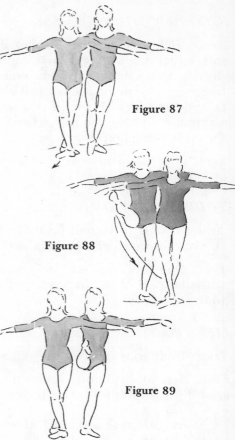

Figure 87

BATTEMENT DÉGAGÉ (Fig. 88)

PT Starting position is same as for battement tendu. The movement is the same as for the battement tendu, but the foot is lifted one inch off the floor and the entire movement is done faster.

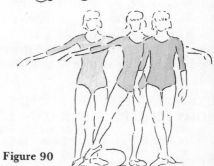

Figure 88

GRAND BATTEMENT (may be done forward, backward or sideward) (Fig. 89)

PT Starting position: Arms in second, feet in fifth (right in front). Slide right foot forward, then lift as high as possible and return to original position. The toe touches the floor first, then the heel touches. The heel pulls the leg back to the original position.

CE 1. Poor body alignment, especially at the hip area.
2. Failure to rotate forward leg outward from the hip.

Figure 89

ROND DE JAMBE A TERRE (en dehors) (Fig. 90)

PT Starting position: Arms in second, feet in first. Begin with plié. Move right foot forward; lift heel and keep toe on floor. Move foot in circular pattern forward and around; then return to original position. Perform eight circles front, then eight circles back, then switch legs.

CE 1. Allowing working knee to relax.
2. Not enough outward hip rotation.

Figure 90

GRAND ROND DE JAMBE EN L'AIR (en dehors) (Fig. 91)

Figure 91

PT Starting position: Arms in second, feet in fifth (right in front). Grand battement with right leg, carry to side, then to the rear. When returning to the original position go through first to a grand battement in front.

CE 1. Poor body alignment.
2. Allowing either leg to bend.
3. Allowing shoulders to move forward or back as the leg circles.

GRAND ROND DE JAMBE EN L'AIR (en dedans) (Fig. 92)

Same as en dehors except that back leg will be lifted to the rear, then forward.

Figure 92

PASSÉ POSITION (Fig. 93)

PT Start in fifth position. With forward foot, draw toe to ankle and up the inside of the leg to the knee. Shift to the back of the knee and slide down the back of the leg to the ankle.

Figure 93

DEVELOPPÉ FORWARD (Fig. 94)

PT Starting position: Arms in second, feet in fifth with right in front. Bring right foot up to knee (to passé position); then extend forward at least 90°. Lower toe to floor and slide back to fifth position.

CE 1. Failure to keep knee of bent leg rotated outward.
2. Extension of forward leg not high enough.
3. Allowing supporting leg (knee) to bend while lifting leg.
4. Allowing supporting hip to relax (sag).

Figure 94

DEVELOPPÉ SIDEWARD (Fig. 95)

Same procedures for developpé forward except that the leg lift is sideways.

Figure 95

ÉCHAPPÉS (Fig. 96)

PT Starting position: Arms in first, feet in fifth, with right in front. Demi-plié, jump to second in demi-plié, return to fifth with same type of jump.

CE 1. Allowing hips to protrude rearward.
2. Failure to keep knees turned outward.

Figure 96

ASSEMBLÉ (Fig. 97)

PT Starting position: Arms in first, legs in fifth with right in front. Demi-plié, and slide left foot out to second on the floor. Hop on right foot extending toes, and land in fifth position with left foot in front. Arms move to second position on hop.

Figure 97

BALLET MOVES THAT CAN BE USED IN FLOOR EXERCISE OR BEAM ROUTINES

The body positions and skills are sometimes varied for use in a gymnastic routine. If the skill starts and ends in the same position, gymnasts, due to the nature of their exercise, will complete only the first half of a skill or will make additional movements.

Example: A gymnast may use the first half of the developpé forward and instead of returning to fifth position will step into another skill.

ATTITUDE (Fig. 98)

PT Start on both feet with body erect. Shift weight to right foot, lift left foot rearward bending the knee outward. Keep upper body erect at all times. The left arm is in fifth position, and the right arm is a little below second. For gymnastics, the arm positions will vary.

Figure 98

ARABESQUE (Fig. 99)

Figure 99

PT Start with weight on both feet and body erect. Shift weight to the right foot, and lift left leg (straight) rearward turned out from the hip. As the left leg is lifted as high as possible, the upper body will have a slight forward lean. Arms may be in second; in opposition; left arm to side of the left leg, right arm forward; or both arms forward, one slightly lower than the other.

CE 1. Allowing the upper body to bend while leg is being lifted in rear.

CHANGEMENT (Fig. 100)

PT Starting position: Arms are in first or second position; the feet are in fifth with the right in front. Plié, then spring upward, and land in fifth position with left foot in front.

Figure 100

JETÉ (Fig. 101)

Figure 101

PT Starting position: Arms in second position, legs in fifth position facing forward. Demi-plié, leap forward, slide left foot to second position with straight knees, spring to left foot from the right foot. Sur le coup de pied in back. Alternate from side to side moving forward.

BALANCÉ (Fig. 102)

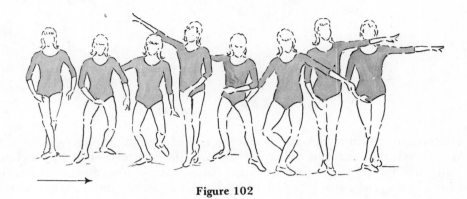

Figure 102

PT Starting position: Arms start in first position and move to second, then back to the first; legs are in fifth position. From the fifth position, the right foot in front, step on a diagonal and step left foot forward to close to fifth position behind the right. Step right in place. May be done forward or back.

GLISSADE (Fig. 103)

Figure 103

PT Starting position: Arms in second, feet in fifth. Slide back foot to second position and close front foot to fifth. Movement is very similar to that of slide when stepping and shifting weight. Arms move from first to second, then return to first.

PAS DE CHAT (sideward) (Fig. 104)

Figure 104

PT Starting position: Arms in second, feet in fifth, left in front. Lift forward foot through passé position (heel in, knee out). Spring onto left foot, and allow the right leg to pass through the bent leg position before landing in back of the left in fifth.

CE 1. Failure to keep knees turned out as far as possible.
2. Failure to keep upper body erect.
3. Failure to go through passé position.

PAS DE CHAT (forward) (cat leap) (Fig. 105)

Figure 105

This is used more in gymnastics then the regular pas de chat. Usually preceded by a step.

PT Starting position: Feet together (arms in second). Step onto right foot; bend left leg lifting knee (through developpé position). Spring onto left foot while lifting and bending right leg. Arms go to first position while body is suspended and return to second as foot contacts floor. Step onto right foot.

CE 1. Insufficient knee bend.
2. Allowing body to lean forward or backward.
3. Failure to keep heels inward of knees.

CABRIOLE (forward) (sometimes called a Hitch Kick) (Fig. 106)

PT Starting position: Feet in fifth (left in front, arms in second. Step forward on left foot, demi-plie. Thrust right leg to 90° angle upward. Bring left leg up to right leg, and have calf of right contact shin of left leg. Lower left foot to floor and return right foot upward to at least a 90° angle. The upper body leans slightly backward as the legs make contact. Reverse movement for back cabriole.

Figure 106

CE 1. Allowing right (top) foot to be lowered to contact left (bottom).
2. Failure to keep legs straight while suspended.

SISSONE (back closed) (Fig. 107)

Starting position: Right arm forward and left in second. Legs in fifth with right foot in front.

PT Plié on both knees and spring diagonally backward on left foot while right foot is raised in front. Land on left foot and drop right to front fifth position in a plié.

Figure 107

SISSONE *(forward closed)* (Fig. 108)

Reverse the movements for the back sissone in closed position.

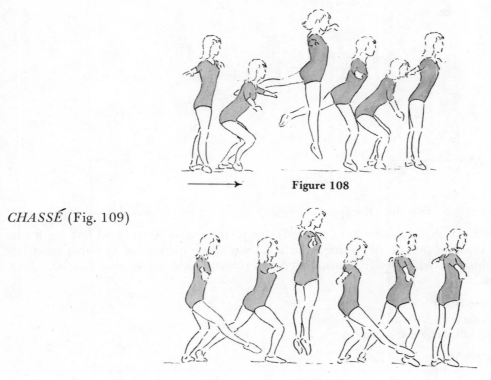

Figure 108

CHASSÉ (Fig. 109)

Figure 109

PT Starting position: Arms in second, feet in fifth with right in front. Demi-plié on left foot as right foot steps forward. Demi-plié on right, springing off of the floor and bringing the left leg to contact the back of the right leg. Land on the left foot. (Same movement principles as for slide and gallop only performed forward.)

CE Allowing the rear foot to pass the forward foot.

CHAINÉ (small turns done in a straight line or on a diagonal) (Fig. 110)

Figure 110

PT In moving left, step left and start turning; step right beside the left foot and finish one full (360°) turn. The arms move to second on the step and slightly close to low fifth (slightly below waist curved in front of body) on the completion of the turn. Eyes should spot an object to the left and maintain that focus as long as possible. Chainés should be practiced on the half toe.

PIQUÉ BACK (Fig. 111)

Figure 111

PT Stand on the right foot with the left raised on the back of the right calf. Step back on the left foot. Turn 360° to the left with right foot on calf of left leg.

PIROUETTE (Fig. 112)

Figure 112

PT From fifth position with the left foot in front. Step on the left, inward rond de jambe on right, and throw left arm outward for speed. Do one or more spins on the left. Just before completion of the turn, drop the right foot in front of the left and pivot as the turn is finished. Keep arms close to first during turn.

TOUR JETÉ (from glissade forward) (Fig. 113)

Refer to balance beam chapter for descriptions.

Figure 113

TOUR JETÉ (from glissade backward) (Fig. 114)

Figure 114

MODERN DANCE AND JAZZ MOVES

A gymnast can show her creative ability by using the modern dance and jazz moves for connecting sequences in her floor exercise routine. These moves are usually in the form of locomotor skill variations and static positions. However, it is suggested that these forms of dance not dominate the routine.

LOCOMOTOR SKILL VARIATIONS (For other variations refer to Chapter 1).

SCISSORS KICK (preceded by a step) (Fig. 115) (Sometimes called a hitch kick)

PT   Step onto the left foot and kick the right leg up as high as possible. As right leg begins downward motion, force the left leg upward. Land on the right foot. Keep arms in second position throughout the skill.

CE   1.   Failure to keep upper body erect.
2.   Failure to switch legs in air.

Figure 115

CABRIOLE FORWARD WITH BENT LEGS (Fig. 116)

PT   Step onto right foot and kick the left foot up as high as possible. Lift the right foot up to touch the left. At this point both legs bend with knees turned out, and contact is made with the toes. Lean upper body slightly backward as the toes contact. As the right foot returns to the floor, straighten left leg and return upward. Arms are in second position throughout the skill.

Figure 116

CE 1. Insufficient thrust of first foot.
2. Failure to allow upper body to lean slightly backward when toes contact.

CANCAN KICK BACKWARD FROM KNEES (Fig. 117)

PT Keeping upper body straight or with very slight forward lean, bend right leg and kick backupward. As the right leg is returning to the floor, bend the left knee and kick backupward. *Keep knees together on kicks.* Keep arms in second position.

Figure 117

STEP SLIDE

A. *Leg forward* (Fig. 118)

Figure 118

PT From a chasse´ or other locomotor skill, step onto right foot (bending knee) and kick left leg forward and upward as high as possible. As left leg is kicking, allow the upper body to lean backward, and extend right leg to allow body to be lifted so that only the toes of the right foot remain on the floor for the sliding action. When momentum is lost, come down on sliding foot, and allow upper body to move forward and go into another skill.

B. *Leg sideward* (Fig. 119)

Figure 119

PT Same principles as leg forward except that the forward leg kicks to the side.

C. *Both legs bent* (Fig. 120)

Figure 120

PT Same principles as above. Body is in croisé position or the step hop position (as described in Chapter I) with both legs bent.

CE (For A, B, and C)
1. Insufficient kick with the forward leg.
2. Failure to extend the back leg to lift the body weight up so that the toe of the front foot can slide freely.
3. Failure to lean body backward on slide.

HOP, STEP HOP (Fig. 121)

Figure 121

PT Step onto the left foot, lift the right knee to the chest, curl the upper body forward over the knee and hop on the left foot. Arms are obliquely backward. Step forward on the right foot (directly from tucked position), lift the upper body, bring arms forward and up to a forward oblique position, and hop on the right foot keeping the left leg extended in the rear and off of the floor.

JUMP WITH BENT LEGS REARWARD (Fig. 122)

PT Spring vertically keeping the upper body (from knees up) in a straight line. Bend the legs as the feet leave the floor and lift the arms to a forward horizontal position.

CE Allowing the hips to flex.

VA During jump, execute 180° turn.

Figure 122

SIDE STEP AND KICK (Fig. 123)

Figure 123

PT Moving sideways, step with the left foot to the left; step behind the left foot with the right; quickly step left with the left foot; then step in front of the left with the right. Swing the left leg sideways and upward as the right arm moves to second and the left arm is down to the side of the body in front of the left leg.

Count: 1-2 and 3-4

       1 step, 2 step back, and step, 3 step front, 4 kick
         l   r   l   r   l

STEP HOP KICK TO A SEMI-SQUAT POSE (Fig. 124)

Figure 124

PT Step on a diagonal with the right foot; kick the left leg upward as a hop is executed forward and upward on the right foot. While in the air, the body is leaning slightly backward. Land with feet together, knees and hips slightly flexed, and upper body directly over the feet. On the jump, keep arms in second position; on landing, move them alongside the body (natural hanging position), with the wrists flexed and fingers pointing outward.

SCHOTTISCHE STEP (Fig. 125)

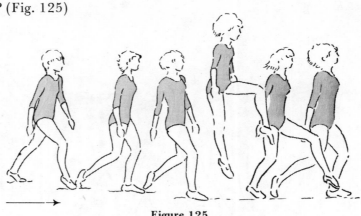

Figure 125

PT   Run right, run left, run right, and hop right.

POLKA STEP (Fig. 126)

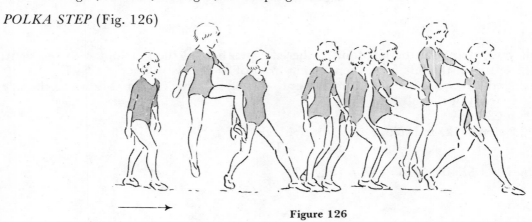

Figure 126

PT   Hop on left, step forward on right, step beside the right with the left foot, and step forward with the right.

Note: The schottische and polka step may be used for variations of movement into a tumbling sequence.

MOVES AND STATIC POSITIONS   (Refer to Chapter IV on the balance beam for other static positions).

BODY WAVE (Fig. 127)

PT   Assume a squat position on the floor with the arms horizontally forward, palms down; turn the palms up, slightly flex the elbows, and move the arms downward and backward to an oblique position. Bring arms forward overhead as the body comes to an erect position. Force the knees forward, straighten the legs pushing the hips forward, arch the back (keeping the shoulders back), and then hunch the shoulders slightly forward as the legs straighten completely.

Figure 127

Note: Arms move with body movement upward.

ROLL TO BODY ARCH FROM PRONE POSITION (Fig. 128)

PT From a prone position on the floor with the arms bent and hands just outside the shoulder, lift the left leg from the knee (upper part of leg remaining on floor), roll over on the right side, extending the left arm and place the left foot on the floor by the right knee. Use the right hand to push the upper body to a sitting position, and slide the right hand close to the hip. When the body reaches the sitting position, move left arm to a forward horizontal position. Extend the hips so that the body is arched and supported on the right hand and the right and left feet. Move left arm to an overhead position. Return to a sitting position, and go into a seat spin, into a backward roll, or execute a valdez.

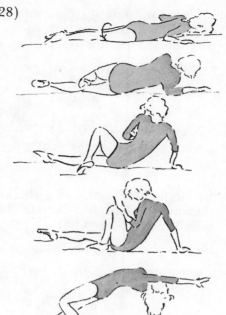

Figure 128

STEP HOP, KICK TO KNEE POSITION ON THE FLOOR (Fig. 129)

PT Step onto the right foot and hop on the right while lifting the left leg forward and upward. As the right foot contacts the floor from the hop, bend the left leg, and move it past the right leg to a kneeling position on the floor. Bend right knee as left leg is placed on the floor. Keep arms in second position or in opposition to the legs.

Figure 129

KNEE SPIN (Fig. 130)

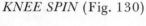

Figure 130

PT Kneel on right knee with left leg bent (at right angles to foot and floor). Turn toward the right. As the body has completed a quarter turn (90°), place the left knee on the floor, and lift right knee and foot from the floor (keeping it bent). Spin 270° right on the left knee to complete the full (360°) turn. Upon completion of the turn, place the right foot on the floor with the knee bent at right angles to the body. *Do not allow the hips to flex on any part of the turn.*

Arms: To begin, bring the right arm (parallel to floor) across the body to the left side. As the turn begins, force the right arm to the right to assist with the spin. The left arm remains in second position and slightly to the front of the body.

SEAT SPIN (Fig. 131)

Figure 131

PT Sitting on the floor, bring the knees to the chest and lean toward the direction of the turn allowing the hands to initiate the spin. Turn the head and shoulders in the direction of the spin. Turn 180° or 360°.

VA May have one leg extended (as in V seat) and the other leg bent (Fig. 131)

BACK SPIN WITH LEG CIRCLING FROM SPLIT POSITION (right leg in back) (Fig. 132)

Figure 132

PT From a deep split position swing the right leg forward to an inverted position as the body rolls onto the back. Keeping the legs as wide apart as possible, make a large circle. As the left leg goes to an inverted position, bend the right leg, and come to a kneeling position; then stand or execute another skill from this position.

STATIC POSITIONS (Fig. 133)

Figure 133

Just by changing the arm or leg positions in many of the standard poses, a different effect may be created. Instead of having palms down or wrists extended, try turning the palms up on some poses and flexing the wrists on others.

Remember that not everyone looks good performing the same pose because of various body types.

Use a full length mirror and try to find the static positions that are most becoming to you as an individual and ones that will achieve the desired effect. Be original.

Transitional Moves and Combinations

BEGINNINGS

1. Fig. 134.

Figure 134

Start in corner 1, facing corner 3. Forcefully extend right leg to rear while lifting body to left toe. Have arms from fifth position to an overhead oblique position. Hesitate momentarily; then run, hurdle and execute a fast tumbling pass toward corner 3.

Music: Fast, dynamic, and continual.

2. Fig. 135.

Figure 135

Stand in corner 1, facing corner 1. As music begins, shift weight on left forward leg, right leg extended to rear with toe on floor. Right arm obliquely foreupward and left arm forward horizontal. Bend left knee and then extend it as the body makes half (180°) turn. (Saute or supersole.) Arms pass through downsideward position to original position on turn. Step, tap, leap, step, pivot turn 180° on left bringing right foot to left, and execute back handspring stepout to a lunge.

Music: Mazurka portion from "Coppelia."

3. Fig. 136.

Figure 136

Start in middle of area facing between corners 3 and 4. After music begins, jump and land sitting on heels with upper body leaning forward over the knees, arms obliquely back. Forcefully lift upper body and place right foot (toe) on floor to the right, body weight supported by left leg; right arm overhead and left arm forward. Make 90° turn to left while lowering right knee to floor and raising left knee (left toe still on floor). Reverse arm position by going through second position. Perform forward roll without hands with right arm leading under left leg. Come to squat, make 180° turn right, and perform a split jump. Land in semi-squat position, twist body from left to right, take three running steps, and slide forward with other leg forward and upward.

Music: *Asia Minor.*

4. Fig. 137.

Figure 137

Stand about ten feet in from corner 2 facing corner 3; place arms at sides and feet together. Perform a C jump; step into lunge; then execute forward roll without hands to the knee, then to split. Make 180° turn in seat spin, pause momentarily, and perform valdez.

5. Fig. 138.

Figure 138

Stand in middle of floor exercise area. Step and execute jump turn 360° on right while lifting left leg at 90° angle from hip (parallel to floor). Land on both feet. Immediately perform back handspring to split. Lift upper body over back knee, stand, step into piquette turn and pose. Run, run, leap, step, two chainé turns, and pose.

Note: The five above sequences have been described from various positions on the floor so that the readers will realize that not all floor exercises must start from any particular part of the 12 x 12 meter area. The suggested music is only for those movements described and is just an example of the types of music that can be used. It is highly recommended that the desired music be improvised and that students not use one song or piece of music in its entirety because they were not written for this purpose. The above sequences may also be used as passés within a routine rather than as openings.

SEQUENCES FOR ROUTINES

1. Fig. 139.

Figure 139

Chassé, step, step push leap, chaine´ turn (360°), step, cat walk, grand battement, forward roll without hands to stand.

2. Fig. 140.

Figure 140

Run, run, leap, step, semi-squat turn (feet together) 180°, grand battement front walkover.

3. Fig. 141.

Figure 141

Run in a circle (four runs), back cancan kick from the knees, step push leap, step hop, cartwheel.

4. Fig. 142.

Figure 142

Kick turn, arabesque, forward roll, stand pose, step, front cabriole, run, run, stag leap.

5. Fig. 143.

Figure 143

Back walkover, glissade backward, step, tour jeté, open toe turn (360°) run, front handspring.

6. Fig. 144.

Figure 144

Forward roll without hands to the knee, then into splits. Back roll to squat stand, arch jump, step, battement tourney, step scissors kick, step, pose.

7. Fig. 145.

Figure 145

Round-off back hand spring, back handspring step out, lunge pose, arabesque, glissade, step, tour jeté.

8. Fig. 146.

Figure 146

Hop, step hop, run, front handspring step out, forward roll without hands to single leg squat, stand, step cat walk.

9. Fig 147.

Figure 147

Chassé, step, step, turn, back roll from stoop position to knee scale, 90° turn toward extended leg in rear, stand, glissade, step, tour jeté, toe rise with feet together and forward arms overhead, run, front handspring step out.

10. Fig. 148.

Figure 148

Back walkover to arabesque, toe rise with feet together and forward-arms down and obliquely down and back; three runs in a semicircle, to jeté forward, step, open toe turn, step front cabriole with bent legs.

11. Fig. 149.

Figure 149

Chainé turn, piqué turn, run, run, leap, step semi-squat turn (feet together), run backward with the upper body curved forward, toe rise, round-off back handspring.

12. Fig. 150.

Figure 150

Saute, step, back cabriole, step, cartwheel with quarter turn, walkover, step pose.

13. Fig. 151.

Figure 151

Kick turn (battement tourney), step, back cabriole, step, cat walk, grand battement, front walkover (scissor legs), illusion splits to splits.

14. Fig. 152.

Figure 152

Pose, cartwheel with quarter turn, chassé, step cabriole with bent legs, handstand forward roll to knee, knee spin, stand, pose.

15. Fig. 153.

Figure 153

Forward roll to squat position, body wave, step, hop step hop, front limbre, step, pas de chat sideways.

16. Fig. 154.

Figure 154

Side step and kick, 90° turn toward lifted leg, cartwheel with quarter turn, run, run, hurdle, round-off back handspring step out.

17. Fig. 155.

Figure 155

Back handspring to splits, seat spin to back roll, come out in pose, extend leg back, arms up, glissade step tour jeté with half pivot turn immediately upon landing, run, run, step slide.

18. Fig. 156.

Figure 156

Polka step, hurdle front aerial, front walkover, step hop kick to kneeling position on the floor, half turn on knee, cartwheel with quarter turn, step, step hop and jump to a semi-squat pose.

19. Fig. 157.

Figure 157

Balancé right, balancé left, step right on right and execute piqué (360°) turn right, grand battement with left foot upon completion of the turn, chassé, step, cat walk, front limbre (or walkover).

20. Fig. 158.

Figure 158

Front handspring to straddle seat, seat spin (360°), valdez, half turn, run, run, run, step slide, step push leap.

Routine Composition for Class

Mass floor exercise seems to be the answer to involving large classes in the floor exercise event. Due to limited space in most schools, the floor pattern and duration of the exercise will probably have to be altered from that of competitive requirements.

Mass floor exercise should involve more dance and locomotor skills than tumbling moves since the routine will be performed on the floor without a regulation mat.

This type of activity assists in developing grace, poise, and rhythm along with an introduction to dance and locomotor skills. The students will also gain an appreciation for and understanding of the event when performed by an advanced gymnast in competition.

These routines can be created in advance or can be a class project. If your background in dance is limited, take advantage of those students in your classes who have had training in dance. Students enjoy the opportunity to assist in composition. Also, *some* of the compulsory routines could be used even if, by modification, a few of the tumbling skills were omitted. Compulsory routines can be found in the DGWS Gymnastic Guide, AAU Handbook, or USGF Handbook.

NOTES

CHAPTER FOUR
BALANCE BEAM

The scope of imagination and creative capacity that enhances balance beam performance is unlimited. This four-inch-wide, sixteen-foot-long piece of apparatus presents a challenge to the student because much body control and courage must be exhibited to manuever the body through the intricacies of the skills and routines performed on the beam. A few years ago one would not believe that girls would even think of performing aerial cartwheels on the beam, but conquering this and similar skills are now a must for a gymnast with international competitive desires.

It is advisable that students practice all skills on the floor (preferably on a line) first to develop proper technique. The skills should next be practiced on a low beam to develop confidence, then finally on a beam of regulation height. In a class situation where you have so many body types and levels of ability, it is suggested that students work and be graded on a *low* beam. This will eliminate a great deal of fear, and students with lesser abilities will find more success. The low beam is also safer and will require less teacher supervision. Skills on the beam will be divided into the following categories:

> Mounts
> Locomotor skills
> Turns
> Static positions
> Tumbling and acrobatic moves
> Dismounts

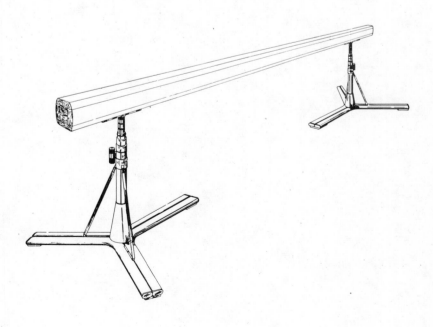

General Safety Hints

1. Students should not be allowed on the equipment unless supervised.
2. Surround the beam with mats.
3. Check before each class period to make sure beam is secure in its supports.
4. Use safety aids, such as beam training pads, for certain skills if possible.
5. Spotters should be alert at all times to avoid accidents. Whenever possible, arrange to have certain students informed in advance of spotting techniques.
6. Avoid mounting the beam around the supports (exceptions being when mounts are performed from the end of the beam).
7. Tell students to get off of the beam when fatigued in order to avoid accidents.
8. If the reuther board is used to mount the beam, it should be removed as soon as the performer is on the beam and out of the way. If the students are just practicing mounts, the board does not have to be moved each time.
9. Wear nonconstrictive clothing and proper footwear.
10. Have a definite skill progression designed for each class.

NOTE: In the following skills, where certain parts of the body have been designated, such as "the right foot," it has been done only for ease of clarification.

Mounts

FRONT SUPPORT TO STRADDLE SEAT (Fig. 159)

Figure 159

PT Stand facing beam (toward middle); place both hands across the beam with fingertips facing away from the body. Jump to a front support with straight arms, upper thighs resting on beam. As the right leg is lifted sideways, up and across the beam to a straddle position, shift the weight to the right hand and turn the left hand across the beam so that the heels of the hands are together. Then lift left leg to complete the straddle position on the beam.

Hint: To learn, allow the legs to lower to the side of the beam and move directly into the straddle sitting position. When more abdominal strength is developed and confidence is gained, maintain legs in wide straddle position as above.

SP Stand on opposite side of the beam; hold upper arms while in a front support to help support and control the performer.

CE 1. Failure to allow shoulders to move forward of the hand position on the beam.
2. Failure to maintain straight arm and leg position throughout mount.
3. Failure to shift weight to one hand when going into straddle position.

MO 1. V-seat: Place both hands on beam behind the body and lift the legs forward and upward. Do not allow the head and shoulders to slump.
2. To squat position: While leaning forward and shifting weight to hands, swing legs down-backward, then upward to a squat position on the beam with one foot slightly in front of the other. Eyes spot end of beam throughout movement.

CE 1. Failure to keep arms straight on backswing of legs before feet are placed on the beam in a squat position.

2. Failure to lean forward (shoulders over hands) throughout backswing.
3. Failure to lift the heels higher than the hips on the backswing before the squat position.

KNEE SCALE MOUNT (Fig. 160)

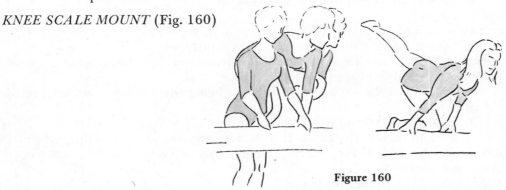

Figure 160

PT Stand facing the beam; place both hands across the beam. Jump to a straight arm support while simultaneously placing the right knee (not shin) on the beam. Left leg is extended to the rear. When springing upward to straight arm support, allow the shoulders to be forward of the hand position. For full extension of the knee scale, change the hands to the opposite grip (finger pointing toward feet), keep shoulders and head up, and fully extend the left leg to the rear.

SP Stand to opposite side of beam. Support upper arm and hip area.

CE 1. Failure to use spring from legs for getting into knee position on the beam.
2. Failure to allow shoulders to lean forward of the hands on the jump to the straight arm support.
3. Failure to maintain straight arms in a knee scale position.
4. Failure to keep head and shoulders up.

MO Quarter (90°) turn right or left on knee to knee scale parallel to length of beam; pose, then stand.

VA Use reuther board placed perpendicular to the beam. Take a running approach into the knee scale mount.

SQUAT MOUNT (Fig. 161)

Figure 161

PT Stand facing beam with hands across the top of the beam. Jump to straight arm support allowing the shoulders to move slightly forward of the hand position. Lift knees to chest, then land on beam with both feet between hands in a deep squat position. Head should be held up at all times.

SP Stand on opposite side of beam and support upper arms, or stand to side of performer and grasp upper arm with inside hand and back of upper leg during the squatting action.

CE 1. Failure to maintain straight arm position.
2. Jumping into rather than up and onto the beam.
3. Failure to keep hips low when squatting.

MO 1. Quarter (90°) right or left into pose.
2. Quarter (90°) turn right or left into forward roll.
3. Stand, quarter (90°) turn right or left into a pose or other locomotor skill.

VA Single leg squat mount.

WOLF MOUNT (Fig. 162)

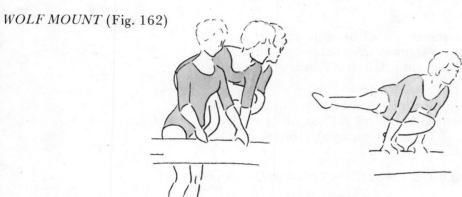

Figure 162

PT Stand facing the beam with hands across the beam. Jump to straight arm support while lifting one knee to chest; then put foot on beam between hands and lift the other leg (straight) to the side of the body and parallel to the beam. Keep the hips low and the shoulders slightly forward and up. The head should be forward and up at all times.

Hint: To learn this mount, allow the toes of the extended leg to rest on the beam; eventually the extended leg should not come in contact with the beam.

SP Stand on opposite side of beam and support upper arms of the performer, or spot one arm and squatting leg.

CE 1. Failure to maintain straight arms.
2. Failure to allow shoulders to move slightly forward of the hand position when jumping onto the beam.
3. Failure to tuck one leg and extend the other leg to the side simultaneously.
4. Failure to keep the extended leg straight.

MO 1. Right leg bent. Quarter (90°) turn right into deep lunge, then stand or perform forward roll.
2. Right leg bent. Quarter (90°) turn left to pose, then stand and   inue.

VA Use reuther board, placing it perpendicular to the beam.

STRADDLE MOUNT (Fig. 163)

PT Jump to straight arm support, allowing shoulders to move slightly forward of the hand position while simultaneously extending the legs sideways in a wide straddle position. Head should be held up and forward.

SP Stand on opposite side of the beam and support the upper arms.

Figure 163

CE 1. Failure to keep arms straight.
     2. Failure to allow the shoulders to lean forward of the hand position.
     3. Failure to lift the hips high enough to allow the legs to remain straight and for placement on the beam.

MO Quarter (90°) turn right or left into a lunge position; then stand or go into a forward roll.

VA 1. Use reuther board placed perpendicular to the beam.
     2. *Free aerial straddle* (Fig. 164).

Figure 164

    PT Same general procedures as for the straddle mount except that the feet do not touch the beam; instead, allow them to pass over the beam and maintain a straddle position across it.

    SP One spotter on opposite side of beam to support upper arms. Second spotter steps in from behind performer to make sure she does not fall backward as her legs straddle.

    MO Quarter (90°) turn maintaining straddle position; sit, go into V seat, then into backward roll, or swing the legs downbackward and upward to a squat position on the beam.

SINGLE LEG SHOOT THROUGH TO STRIDE LEG POSITION (Fig. 165)

Figure 165

PT Place hands across beam. Jump to straight arm support while simultaneously lifting the hips high enough to allow one leg to bend; bring knee to the chest; then extend leg forward across the beam. Other leg remains straight at all times. Keep the head and shoulders forward and up.

SP Stand beside performer's shoot-through leg, grasp upper arm, and support throughout skill.

CE 1. Failure to maintain straight arms.
     2. Failure to allow shoulders to move forward of the hand position.
     3. Failure to elevate the hips high enough to allow one leg to bend and pass over the beam.
     4. Failure to follow through with shoot leg (extend knee and thrust leg forward).
     5. Allowing shoot-through knee to turn outward rather than lifting it directly toward the chest.

MO 1. Rest on beam in stride position, quarter (90°) turn to a V seat.
     2. Rest on beam, quarter (90°) turn, backward roll.
     3. Rest on beam, quarter (90°) turn, swing legs downbackward and upward to squat position on beam.

FORWARD ROLL MOUNT (usually done with reuther board placed at end of beam) (Fig. 166)

Hips not up high enough

Figure 166

PT At the end of the beam place both hands on the beam with the heels of the hands facing each other. While springing from feet, extend arms; elevate hips high enough to be able to tuck head and to place the back of the neck and upper back on the beam. When neck and upper back have contacted the beam, immediately shift the hands to the bottom of the beam. Keep the elbows close to the head and pull with the hands to maintain balance. Keep body in piked position and lower body to beam as if trying to make each vertebra contact the beam, one after the other.

SP One spotter on each side of the beam. One standing beside performer to keep her in the inverted position by lifting her thighs to get hips overhead. Second spotter helps lower body to beam by grasping performer's waist. Second spotter stands to back of performer as she is rolling.

CE 1. Failure to maintain straight arm support and to allow the hips to get high enough to tuck the head.
2. Not tucking the head soon enough.
3. Failure to transfer hands to bottom on beam and to pull to help maintain balance.
4. Failure to remain in pike position while lowering body to beam.

MO 1. To V-seat position.
2. Roll to squat stand; immediately stand.
3. Roll to crotch (straddle) seat position; swing legs downbackward and upward to a squat stand on beam.
4. Roll to squat stand, pose, then stand.

VA 1. *Forward roll to lever* (Fig. 167)

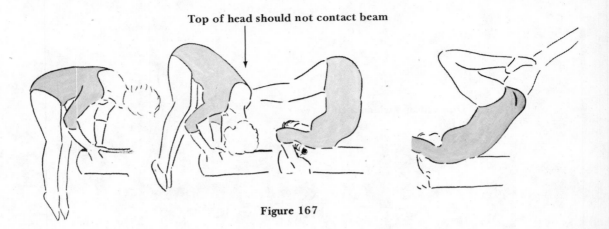

Top of head should not contact beam

Figure 167

PT Same preparation as for regular forward roll mount; after tucking head and lowering back of neck and upper shoulders to beam, extend body (hips foreupward and legs foreupward and down) to lever position, then continue to roll.

2. *Swing forward roll* (Fig. 168)

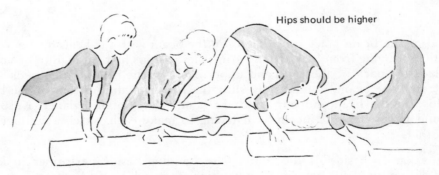

Hips should be higher

Figure 168

PT Jump to front rest support on end of beam (hands across beam with heel of hands toward each other). Immediately swing legs forward and upward to a straddle position. Allow shoulders to move forward of the hand position as the legs forcefully swing down-backward and upward. Lift hips; tuck head, lowering upper shoulders to beam; shift hands to bottom of beam; then continue to roll.

SP Spot same as for forward roll mount on beam.

STEP ON MOUNT (usually done obliquely to or at end of beam) (Fig. 169)

Figure 169

PT After approaching the beam from an angle, swing the inside leg foreupward onto the beam, followed by the outside leg. (Leg action is very similar to the scissors kick in the high jump.) Put second foot on the beam slightly in front of the first. Extend legs when kicking but immediately tuck in order to land in a squat position. Upper body must be slightly forward to allow momentum to carry the body up onto the beam. Keep eyes focused forward and upward.

Hint: To learn this, use the hand closest to the beam until in a squat position. Eventually the hand should not come in contact with the beam.

SP 1. Hold outside hand of performer and run with her giving assistance on the jump.
    2. Stand on the opposite side of the beam and reach across the beam to grasp the performer's inside hand and upper arm.

CE 1. Failure to use one-foot take-off.
    2. Failure to swing the inside leg vigorously foreupward.
    3. Failure to keep momentum going forward by slightly leaning into the jump.
    4. Trying to stand too soon on the beam after reaching the squat position.

MO 1. Immediately stand after balance is attained in the squat position.
    2. Pose, then stand.
    3. Forward roll.
    4. High squat jump.

VA *At end of beam* (Fig. 170)

Figure 170

PT From a running approach and one-foot take-off, spring vertically and step onto the end of the beam. The foot that makes first contact with the beam is the foot that did not make contact with the reuther board. The second foot doesn't usually touch the beam until a static position has been shown.

HALF TURN STRADDLE MOUNT ON END OF BEAM (Fig. 171)

Figure 171

PT Learn on lower beam then raise beam and use reuther board. With a two foot take-off, grasp end of beam with both hands, arms extended. Immediately make a half turn left while removing left hand from beam. As body comes to sitting position on beam, right hand may be placed on beam in front of body for support.

SP Grasp waist area and assist in the lift and turn.

CE 1. Not jumping high enough before turning.
2. Removing left hand too late.

MO 1. Backward roll.
2. V seat; then swing legs downward and upward to squat stand.

HANDSTAND MOUNT using reuther board perpendicular to beam (Fig. 172)

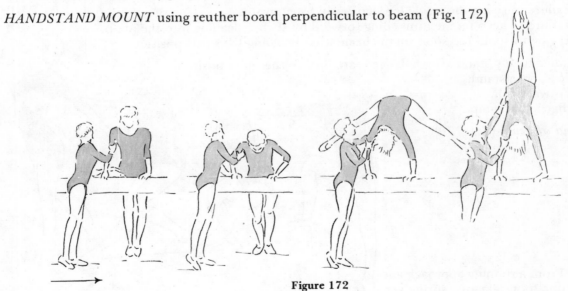

Figure 172

PT Run and place hands across beam. Jump to straight-arm support while simultaneously raising hips overhead (inverted position). Keep arms and shoulders extended at all times. When hips are over hands, shoulders will be slightly forward of hands. At this time extend harder in shoulders, pulling them back. Continue lifting legs to handstand position.

SP Stand in front of performer on opposite side of beam. Grasp hips and help them overhead. (May have to stand on something to be high enough; or keep beam very low.)

CE 1. Failure to maintain straight-arm support.
2. Failure to spring enough to attain inverted position.
3. Failure to keep hips overhead while lifting legs overhead.
4. Failure to keep head tilted backward and to spot a stationary object in front of the body.

MO 1. Stoop down to beam, quarter turn, pose.
2. Straddle down to beam and use any suggestion given for movement out of straddle mount.
3. Quarter turn to English handstand and forward roll.
4. Quarter turn to English handstand and swing down or chest roll.
5. Stoop through to V-sit crossways on beam, quarter turn and backward roll.
Hint: Should master a press handstand on floor before attempting this skill on beam.

HANDSTAND MOUNT ON END OF BEAM (Fig. 173)

Figure 173

PT From run and two-foot takeoff on reuther board, punch board as if vaulting and place hands on end of beam. Drive hips upward keeping arms straight with head up (eyes looking in front of hands), legs staying close to the body in a straddle position. When hips are over hands, extend legs upward to a completely stretched handstand position. At all times keep shoulders over hands and do not allow back to arch.

SP Two spotters in the beginning. Stand on floor beside board and beam. As performer takes off board, grasp upper arm with near hand and hip area with far hand. Steady arm and assist with lift in hip area. One spotter could stand on a solid object at side of beam and grasp waist area as hips are coming over shoulder position.

MO 1. Forward roll
2. Walkover
3. Pirouette

Locomotor Skills

Locomotor skills are a major part of balance-beam performance; however, they are mainly used as transitional and contrasting moves. These skills must be practiced individually, but when a routine is being composed, there must be continuity from one skill to the next. The following skills should be practiced on the floor first, then transferred to the beam. Since most of the skills have been previously discussed in Chapter I, only information pertinent to the balance beam will be mentioned.

Spotting for most locomotor skills is usually done to the side of the beam. The spotter walks along with or stands by the performer and offers an outstretched hand at all times, so that she may assist in maintaining balance or prevent a fall. It is very important for the spotter to know what skills are being performed and to be alert at all times.

WALKS

FORWARD WALK

PT Stand with body erect, abdominals tense, hips tucked under body. Lead with the toe, leg slightly turned out from hip. Arms hold definite position. Take small, rather than large, steps. Eyes spot end of beam (*never* look at feet) or stationary object at eye level.

CE 1. Walking flat footed.
2. Body posture incorrect.
3. Taking too large or too small a step.
4. Body too tense.
5. Allowing arms to dangle.

MO Usually not more than one or two walking steps are made at one time in a beam routine, so almost any of the tumbling skills, poses, and other locomotor skills can be done out of the walks.

VA 1. Walk high and low with various combinations.
2. Walk backward, allowing the foot to extend to the side of the beam as it is moving to the beam in back of the body.
3. Increase speed of walk and gradually develop into a run.

HOPS, LEAPS, AND JUMPS

These locomotor skills should be learned on the floor first because they require the body be momentarily lifted above the beam. Toes leave the beam last when taking off and contact the beam first when landing. These skills are always started in a semi-plié (slight knee bend with heel off of beam) position and ended in a semi-plié or some other position that allows for flexion of the knees to absorb shock, allows for smooth landing, and assists in maintaining balance. The upper body is almost always held erect except in skills used to convey certain body lines. The arms should be soft and flowing and also used to assist in gaining or giving the impression of attained height. When the leg goes backward in a certain skill, it is turned out from the hips rather than extended directly backward.

It is very important that hops, leaps, and jumps be explosive and show maximum height and full body extension. If the skills are to be used for height, the movement must start and end in the same vertical plane; if they are to be used for distance, then loss of balance forward should occur before movement is taken forward and upward.

When spotting, stand to side of beam and offer outstretched hand to performer at all times.

Suggested combinations of locomotor skills (foot and arm positions should be reversed so performer will not become onesided).
1. Step, step hop, run, run, jump into deep squat.
    r   l   r   l   slightly in front of l.
2. Grand battement forward, changement, slide, step, cat walk.
                r   r in front   l   l   start with r
3. Run, run, regular leap, run, run, stag leap.
        l   r   l   r   l   r
4. Step, cat walk, step hop, extend forward leg, 2 steps
    r   start l   r   l   l,r
backward, squat jump.

Turns and Pirouettes

Turns are used on the balance beam to change direction and add variety to a routine. They should be done high on the balls on the feet except in variations. The body should be held erect, with the head up, shoulders relaxed. Turns should convey a feeling of lightness and continual motion. For balance, the center of gravity must always be over the base of support (feet). Turns should generally be executed using small steps. Arms should hold a definite position and help lift the body to the balls of the feet when turning. When the leg is lifted in a turn, such as the kick turn, it should be lifted at least parallel to the beam. Eye spotting is very important in turning for balance and to prevent dizziness.

Spotting for turns: Stand at side of beam and assist with outstretched hand.

SQUAT TURN (Fig. 174)

PT   Assume deep squat position on balls of feet with one foot slightly in front of the other and hips directly above feet. Keep shoulders and head up with slight arch in back. Hold arms out at sides. Lift body very slightly and pivot a half turn (180°) on balls of feet. Eye spot other end of beam after turning.

Figure 174

CE 1. Failure to squat with the hips over the heels and maintain this position throughout the turn.
     2. Failure to keep the shoulders directly over the hips.
     3. Allowing the head to tilt forward and down.
     4. Failure to eye spot.

MO 1. Pose, then stand.
     2. Forward roll.
     3. Squat jump.
     4. Immediately stand.

VA *Semi-squat turn* (Fig. 175).

     PT Be careful that upper body does not sag forward. Be conscious of body lines in this position.

Figure 175

PIVOT TURN ON TOES (Fig. 176)

PT   Stand with one foot slightly in front of the other on the balls of the feet. Keep body erect, head up, and shoulders relaxed. Initiate the turn with the hips and shoulders and squeeze the inner thighs or knees together for balance. Pivot, making half (180°) turn and end facing the opposite direction. Arms may be held sideways throughout turn, or have one arm forward in opposition to the front foot and the other arm sideways. Eyes spot other end of beam or some object at eye level after turn.

Figure 176

CE 1. Failure to maintain body erect throughout turn (if body leans forward, backward, or side-ward, loss of balance will occur).
2. Failure to eye spot.
3. Allowing feet to be too far apart on turn.

MO 1. Go into any of the locomotor skills.
2. Pose.
3. Step, kick into English handstand, execute a cartwheel or another tumbling skill.
4. Go into deep squat position and perform an arch jump (for distance).

BATTEMENT TOURNEY (kick turn) (Fig. 177)

PT Kick right leg forward and upward; twist the body to the left and pivot on ball of left foot making half (180°) turn. As the turn is completed, the right leg should be carried up high behind the body. Keep shoulders directly over the left foot throughout the turn for balance; during the twisting action the back must arch to allow the shoulders to remain over the foot. End in a low arabesque, high arabesque, or go directly into another locomotor skill or some other move such as the forward roll. Arms may be in second position or go from a natural hanging position to fifth position as the body twists. Eyes spot stationary object or end of beam.

Figure 177

Note: This turn is usually preceded by a step, chassé, or glissade.

CE 1. Allowing shoulders to move backward on the kick forward and upward.
2. Allowing the shoulders to drop forward after the turn is completed.
3. Failure to lift body and turn on the toes.

VA *Kick hop turn* (Fig. 178)

    PT Perform in the same manner as the kick turn, but have left foot completely leave the beam during the turn.

Figure 178

TOUR JETÉ (Fig. 179)

Figure 179

PT Step on right foot; kick left leg forward and upward. Quickly twist the body a half turn (180°) and land on the left foot, swinging right leg to the rear. Shoulders should not lean forward or backward during the turn. Take arms overhead when the left leg swings forward. Eyes spot end of beam or stationary object after turn is completed.

CE 1. Allowing the shoulders to move backward as right leg swings forward.
    2. Allowing shoulders to move forward after turn and landing on right foot.
    3. Failure to flex right knee slightly upon landing on right foot.

VA Precede tour jeté with a chassé or a glissade.

CHAINÉ TURN (Fig. 180)

Figure 180

PT Step onto left foot; pivot a half turn (180°). Step onto right foot and pivot a half turn (180°) to complete the full turn. Steps are very small and are made on the half toe. Arms usually open to second position on the step and close (not completely) on the completion of the turn. Eye spotting is very important in this turn. When stepping to the left, turn the head to the left and hold this focus as long as possible. As you step on the right foot, turn head at the last second.

CE 1. Leaning into the turns or allowing the shoulders to move backward of the foot.
    2. Poor eye spotting.

Note: When these turns are performed on the beam, usually only one is performed; however, when performed on the floor in floor exercise, they are done in a series. When performed in a series, the same eye focus should be used.

PIROUETTE (Fig. 181)

Figure 181

PT On the beam, the pirouette is usually preceded by a step. It is a fast vertical spin of the body on one foot (tip-toe). The second foot (or free foot) can be held at the ankle, in attitude, or in arabesque position. Allow the body to lean very slightly forward on the turn in order to get up on toes. Arm positions will depend on the position of the second foot.

CE 1. Failure to step into and then lift body vertically onto toes.
    2. Leaning too far forward into the turn and letting the shoulders move too far backward at any time during the turn.

Static Positions

Poses are held only long enough to show that balance has been achieved in that position.

The following are just a few of the many static positions; but the performer will receive more credit for her routine if she can create something original or even vary some of the following.

Figure 182

Tumbling and Acrobatic Moves

FORWARD ROLL (Fig. 183)

Figure 183

PT With one foot slightly in front of the other stretch forward and place both hands across the beam (thumb and heel of hand on top of beam, fingers down side of beam). Shift the weight to the hands while lifting the hips above the head. Keeping the hips forward and upward, start bending elbows, tuck the head, and lower to beam in order to place back of neck and upper shoulder on beam. *Head must go between arms.* As the neck and upper shoulder area contact the beam, immediately shift the hands to the bottom of the beam and squeeze the elbows together (pulling with hands to keep body on beam). Continue rolling forward, slowly, maintaining a pike position as long as possible (should feel as if each vertebrae contacts the beam one after the other). Once learned, the hands need not grasp the bottom of the beam.

Hint: Some people find success starting from the knees on the beam and then going directly into the roll.

SP Stand at side of beam and face performer. As she tucks her head, grasp her hips and help lower her to the beam.

CE 1. Failure to lift hips high enough to allow head to be tucked and placed between arms on the beam.
    2. Failure to keep elbows close together and to pull on bottom of beam after shoulders have been placed on beam and hands switched to the bottom of the beam.
    3. Failure to maintain pike position when rolling on the back.
    4. Rolling too fast.

MO 1. Straddle beam and swing legs downbackward and upward to squat position, or land in a knee scale and go into pose.
    2. To V-sit.
    3. To single leg squat, pose, then stand.
    4. To squat position, pose, then stand.

VA 1. *Forward roll from stoop position* (Fig. 184).

Figure 184

In general, requires better than average flexibility.

2. *Swing forward roll* (Fig. 185).

Figure 185

PT From straddle position, thrust hips upward, simultaneously swinging legs (heels leading) downbackward and upward while shifting weight to hands. Allow hips to become high enough to successfully tuck head and continue rolling.

3. *Forward roll without hands* (Fig. 186).

Figure 186

PT Go into deep lunge, arms out at sides of body and parallel to floor. Lower shoulder and back of neck to beam (constantly look at other end of beam until body on beam) and continue to roll. Arms remain to side of body throughout skill.

BACKWARD ROLL TO SQUAT (Fig. 187)

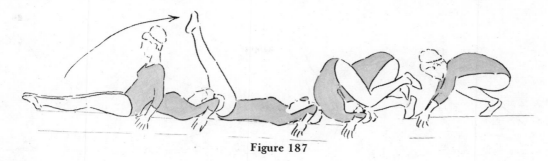

Figure 187

BACK ROLL TO KNEE SCALE

PT Maintain balance in supine position. Place thumbs on top of beam under neck, with fingers on side of beam. Some people prefer both hands on the bottom of the beam in front of the head; some prefer one hand on top and the other hand on the bottom of the beam. Lift legs in a tuck or pike position (should be straight knees eventually) to an overhead position. As the hips pass overhead, extend the arms (push with thumbs and grasp beam with fingers); place foot or feet on the beam and finish in a knee scale, in a squat position, or immediately stand. As soon as the head can be lifted, the performer should eye spot the end of the beam.

SP Two spotters at first, one on each side of the beam. Assist the performer by grasping at the waist or hips as the hips are passing over the head. May also assist placement of the foot or knee on the beam before the roll is completed.

CE 1. Failure to maintain tuck or pike position when rolling.
2. Failure to push with hands as hips pass over head.
3. Failure to eye spot end of beam to assist in maintaining balance.

MO 1. End in squat position, pose.
2. End in squat position, half (180°) turn and pose.
3. End in knee scale, sit back on heel, then stand.
4. End in single leg squat position, pose.
5. *End in knee scale position, pose, then stand* (Fig. 188).

Figure 188

VA 1. Two backward rolls in succession.
2. Backward roll to needle scale.
3. Backward roll to head stand.
4. Backward roll to English handstand.

BACK SHOULDER ROLL (Head to left of beam, rolling over right shoulder) (Fig. 189)

Figure 189

PT From a supine position, place head to side of the beam so that right shoulder is on the beam; adjust balance. Place left hand on top of beam (fingers to side of beam, thumb on top), left arm across neck, and right hand on bottom of beam. Some people prefer to have both hands on the top of the beam. Lift legs to chest in a tuck or pike position and continue rolling over shoulder until head and torso can be lifted upward. The right knee should contact the beam, and the right hand should be shifted to the top of the beam. *Eyes spot end of beam toward shoulder when rolling,* and shift to other end of beam as roll is completed.

SP Same as for backward roll.

CE 1. Failure to stay in a tuck or pike position while rolling backward.
2. Failure to use hands in a push and pull fashion to maintain body on beam (bottom hand pulls, top hand pushes).
3. Failure to constantly eye spot.

MO Same as backward roll.

ENGLISH HANDSTAND (Fig. 190)

PT Lift arms overhead while lifting left leg parallel (or above) to the beam. Step forward onto the left foot bending the knee slightly and supporting the majority of the body weight. Place the hands on the beam (heel of hands together, fingers to side of beam) about eighteen inches in front of the left foot. Shift weight to hands, swing the right leg up, immediately followed by a push from the second leg. When body reaches inverted position, the legs are together and straight, shoulders and hips are fully extended, and the head should be held up and back to allow the eyes to spot the beam at least ten inches in front of the hands.

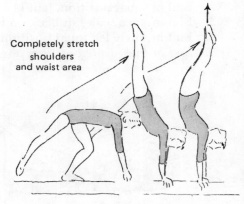

Completely stretch shoulders and waist area

Figure 190

SP Spotters on each side of the beam. One spotter supports upper arms, and the other grasps the hips to support and control the performer. If the handstand is not attained, performer should be told to keep arms straight and shift body weight slightly to one side of the beam and allow feet to be lowered to the floor by the spotter.

CE 1. Failure to maintain straight-arm support.
2. Failure to squeeze the beam with the hands.
3. Too much arch in back.

4. Insufficient swing with first leg, insufficient push with second leg, or both.
5. Failure to extend body fully in inverted position.
6. Failure to keep head up and back.

MO 1. Forward roll (covered on page 95).
   2. *Swing down* (Fig. 191).

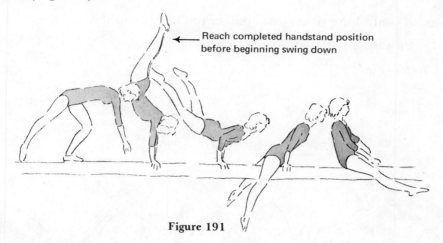

← Reach completed handstand position before beginning swing down

Figure 191

PT   Force the head up and back and shift weight forward over hands, making sure elbows do not bend. Leading with pelvis, lower legs to beam (one to each side) with inside of thighs making contact. As soon as the legs have contacted the beam, the shoulders and head should be lifted up and back while slightly arching the back. As the pelvis is leading downward, the heels must be forced upward.

HANDSTAND FORWARD ROLL (Fig. 192)

Too much arch

Figure 192

PT   After attaining full body extension and balance in the English handstand, shift hips and shoulders backward as if beginning to pike. Control elbow bend and lower body to beam; tuck head and place back of neck and upper shoulder area on the beam between arms. As soon as upper shoulder area contacts the beam, transfer hands to the bottom of the beam. Maintain a pike position and continue to roll.

SP   One spotter supports upper arm and abdomen in the handstand position, and the other grasps the hips to support and maintain control while performer lowers to beam and rolls.

CE 1. Failure to shift hips and shoulders slightly backward when beginning to lower body to beam.
    2. Failure to lower body to beam in the same vertical plane that the handstand was in (shoulders should not move forward of the hands).
    3. Failure to keep legs well behind head (tight pike) momentarily after upper back contacts beam.
    4. Failure to control the elbow bend (either too fast or too slow).

MO Same as for forward roll.

CARTWHEEL (left) (Fig. 193)

Figure 193

PT Lift arms overhead while simultaneously lifting the left leg at least parallel to beam. Step forward onto left foot, bending the knee slightly and shifting the body weight to that leg. Begin swinging the right leg up and immediately place the left hand across the beam (heel of hand toward the center of the beam). Push off the beam with the left leg. Just before the body reaches the inverted position, place the right hand on the beam about five inches in front of the left. The right foot should contact the beam closer to the right hand than in a regular cartwheel on the floor. The right leg should bend slightly upon landing. The left hand should push off the beam slightly before the right foot lands on the beam. Left leg continues as the right leg extends (straighten knee) and the right hand is removed from the beam. After completion of the skill, the entire body should be facing toward the end of the beam. Eyes spot hands on the beam when inverting and look at the end of the beam or stationary object at eye level as the body is raised.

SP Stand beside beam and support second arm placed on beam and waist. If performer is off balance, she should do a round-off dismount to the side of the beam. Spot as if spotting a cartwheel on the floor.

CE 1. Placing hands on beam before beginning kicking action.
    2. Failure to kick legs through vertical plane (many tend to pike).
    3. Failure to step forward and shift the weight to bend forward leg after preparatory leg and arm lift.

4. Failure to place hands fairly close together (when learning).
5. Failure to straighten up immediately after first foot contacts beam. (Students tend to feel that they can maintain balance by staying low and delaying hand releases from the beam; however, their center of gravity is too high to maintain balance, so it is more advantageous to raise upper body as soon as possible.)

MO 1. Go into lunge position.
2. Bring back leg forward and continue walking; or pose; or turn on toes.
3. Go into pose.

VA 1. *One-handed cartwheel (near arm)* (Fig. 194)

Figure 194

2. *One-handed cartwheel (far arm)* (Fig. 195)

Figure 195

FRONT WALKOVER
(Fig. 196)

Figure 196

PT For detailed description refer to tumbling chapter since movement is identical to that on floor, except the hand placement. Hands are placed on beam so that fingers are on side of beam pointing downward and heels of hands toward each other (same as for English handstand). *Master* on line on floor before attempting on beam.

Hint: Sometimes it helps to perform the walkover on the long horse, because the area is a little wider, before going directly from a low beam to a beam of regulation height. The wider base will also help minimize fear of height.

SP Stand facing the performer. With the inside hand (palm up) grasp the upper arm as the performer places her hands on the beam. Outside hand is placed on lower back giving support throughout skill. Spotter should also watch performer's placement of foot on the beam and control it if necessary.

CE Refer to tumbling section.

MO 1. Into pose.
2. Into lunge.
3. Step forward and go into a high pivot turn on both feet.

BACK WALKOVER
(Fig. 197)

Figure 197

PT For details refer to tumbling section. Master on floor first. The back walkover seems to be easier to learn than the front walkover because the eyes can spot the beam and the performer can see where she is going.

SP Stand with back to performer's back. Cock wrists and grasp hip area with thumbs pointing toward each other and fingers grasping outer hip area. As hands contact beam and hips are passing over hands, force wrists in opposite direction to assist in shifting weight past performer's hands.

VA 1. *Back walkover to splits* (refer to tumbling) (Fig. 198)

Figure 198

2. *Back walkover stop in English handstand, then swing down* (Fig. 199)

Figure 199

Dismounts

Landing on all dismounts should be with slight knee bend to absorb shock and to help maintain balance. For safety reasons, it is advisable to have two spotters when first learning most of the dismounts. Make sure there are sufficient mats beside or at the end of the beam where the dismounts will be performed. For the more difficult dismounts use a crash pad.

ARCH JUMP DISMOUNT (Fig. 200)

Figure 200

PT Stand sideways on the beam. Bend knees and spring up and forward. While suspended, *keep upper body erect.* Keep head up and eye spot stationary object at eye level throughout skill.

SP Stand behind beam and performer. Have outstretched hands ready to push performer forward if she should come too close to the beam. Another spotter could stand in front of the performer to prevent her from falling forward.

CE 1. Failure to keep upper body erect.
2. Failure to push off balls of feet in order to gain maximum elevation.
3. Jumping out too far or not far enough.

ENGLISH HANDSTAND DISMOUNT (Fig. 201)

Figure 201

PT Kick up into English handstand balance as described on page 98 (Fig. 190). Slightly shift weight to right side of the beam, slightly flex then extend hips, and thrust legs and feet to the mat (similar to snap down). As feet are coming to right of beam, lift upper body and remove right hand from beam and lift it sideways. Eyes spot beam in front of hands until feet have been forced downward. Shoulders and head are then lifted and eyes spot stationary object (eye level) or end of beam.

Hint: To learn go from a deep lunge position and only kick legs upward to a 45° angle. Action is very similar to front or face vault action.

SP Stand across beam to performer's left, directly in line with performer's hand placement. Place inside hand on upper arm and outside hand on abdomen or left thigh to make sure performer clears the beam. This method enables the spotter to maintain complete control of the performer throughout the entire skill.

CE 1. Not achieving full handstand position before descending.
2. Failure to maintain straight arms throughout dismount.
3. Failure to lift upper body and remove one hand to side as legs make downward movement.
4. Failure to shift body weight to right side of beam so as to land on the mat.

ROUND-OFF (end of beam) (Fig. 202)

Figure 202

PT Stand about two and one-half feet from the end of the beam, facing the end. Lift left leg upward as arms go overhead. Step onto left foot, shifting weight to that foot, and begin swinging right leg backupward. Place both hands together on the beam with fingers (of both hands) going down right side of beam. Push with left foot and bring both legs together in the inverted position. Make a half turn with entire body and pike at hips to allow feet to land on the floor. Push off end of beam with hands after feet have past the inverted position. Eyes spot hand placement on the beam. When feet have contacted the mat and head and shoulders are lifted, eyes spot a stationary object at eye level.

SP Stand to nonturning side of performer, grasp upper arms as they are placed on beam and maintain contact until feet are on mat.

CE 1. Failure to maintain straight arms throughout skill.
2. Not achieving a handstand position before turning.
3. Failure to push off the beam with the hands and eye spot correctly.

VA *Round-off to side of beam* (Fig. 203)

Figure 203

PT If performing on same side as above, student should land on the mat to the right side of the beam. You do not cross the beam on this dismount.

CARTWHEEL (end of beam) (Fig. 204)

Figure 204

PT Same preparatory moves and hand placement as for the round-off. Instead of making a half turn, *make sure that feet come together while inverted and maintain a sideward position* throughout dismount. As body is going past the vertical position, push off with second hand and allow body to "float" to landing position on the mat. Make sure there is no undercutting action (forcing legs under body) with feet upon landing.

SP Stand beside beam at performer's back and support upper arm and hip.

CE 1. Failure to keep arms straight.
      2. Failure to bring legs together when inverted.

3. Piking (flexing hips) while inverted.
4. Failure to push off of the beam with the second hand.
5. Failure to lift the head up immediately upon landing and to eye spot a stationary object at eye level.
6. Allowing legs to undercut.

CARTWHEEL QUARTER TURN DISMOUNT (Fig. 205)

Figure 205

PT Stand approximately three feet from end of beam. Lift arms and right leg. Lunge forward on right bent leg, and place hands on beam to right side (close together) while kicking left leg. Immediately push with right leg to get body to handstand position. When body is sideways and vertical, bring legs together as in cartwheel dismount. As the body continues past the vertical plane, push and release the right hand, turn head to right, and push off with the left hand keeping both arms overhead. Land with back to beam, bending knees and hips slightly to absorb shock.

SP Stand to back of performer and grasp under arm pits after body is on down flight to help keep upper body from falling forward.

CE 1. Too much momentum developed from leg kick and push action causing lack of control and falling forward on landing.
2. Failure to pass through the vertical position causing landing to be off to the side of the beam.
3. Allowing head and upper body to drop forward on landing.

HANDSTAND QUARTER TURN SQUAT (Fig. 206)

Figure 206

PT Kick up into side handstand position while simultaneously making quarter (90°) turn (as if to perform cartwheel). Place hands on the beam with fingertips on the side of the beam and heels of hands on top. After handstand position is achieved, slightly overbalance, maintaining shoulders over hands. (It is very important not to allow the shoulder to move forward of the hands.) As balance is lost, flex hips and knees while simultaneously forcing (lifting) head and chest upward. Extend legs before landing.

Hint: Lead-ups 1. Handstand quarter turn, hold.
                         2. Snap down on floor.

SP Two spotters. One stands on performer's pivot side and supports arm with outside hand; as the performer begins to squat, spotter places inside hand on abdomen. Second spotter stands on nonpivot side of performer. As handstand position is attained, she places outside hand on upper arm and inside hand on abdomen. When performer can achieve handstand position alone, spotters can stand on each side and grasp forearm with outside hand and upper arm with inside hand and help pull performer through squat position and off beam.

CE 1. Failure to achieve proper handstand position (slight overbalance).
       2. Failure to maintain straight arms.
       3. Allowing shoulders to move forward of the hands.
       4. Not following through completely on the squat as it is executed.
       5. Failure to push with hands as squat is executed.
       6. Failure to keep head up.

VA 1. *Handstand stoop through* (Fig. 207)

Figure 207

2. *Handstand straddle off* (Fig. 208).

Figure 208

WINDY (Fig. 209)

Figure 209

PT Arm and leg lift the same as for handstand position. Place right hand on beam, with fingers at right side of beam and heel of hand on beam. Kick up into a one-arm handstand position, keeping the right shoulder over the right hand. Lean body in the direction of the pivot. Make half (180°) turn and allow feet to move toward the mat, keeping body fully extended. As legs are lowering to mat, lift head and upper body forcefully. Eyes spot supporting hand while inverted and end of beam as head and upper body are lifted. Hand remains in contact with the beam until feet contact the mat. Left arm should swing vigorously down, back, and overhead as the skill is initiated.

SP Stand at pivot side of performer. Support upper arm with inside hand and abdomen with outside hand.

CE 1. Failure to achieve handstand position on one arm.
   2. Failure to keep supporting arm straight.
   3. Failure to lean body into the direction of the pivot.
   4. Failure to keep shoulder over supporting hand.
   5. Failure to execute forceful swing and push from the legs.
   6. Failure to use left arm.

Hint: Learn with both hands on the beam.

FRONT AERIAL (end of beam) (Fig. 210)

Figure 210

PT Same technique as for skill on floor (refer to tumbling section for details). Legs are brought together in the inverted position; then toes reach for the mat to allow body to "float" to the mat in a wide arc. Be careful not to allow legs to undercut (pass under body) body before landing.

SP 1. To learn use inside hand on shoulder and outside hand on wrist. Standing at end of beam, move with performer to prevent undercutting.
   2. Inside hand on abdomen, outside hand on small of back.

SIDE AERIAL DISMOUNT (Fig. 211)

Figure 211

PT Lift arms over head and leg up in preparation for step into aerial. Step forward onto bent right foot with toes near end of beam. Keeping head and shoulders erect over right knee, immediately kick the left foot as a push is made with the right foot. As the body moves forward and upward drop the right shoulder so that it is in line with the beam and bring legs together in vertical position. Land with left side to beam, arms overhead, then down, and hips and knees slightly flexed to absorb shock. Eyes focus on object at eye level.

SP 1. Stand to back of performer, place near hand on right side of waist and far hand on left. Same as spotting cartwheel on floor.
2. Place both hands on pelvic area, and lift and assist with rotation when leg thrust is made.

CE 1. Dropping head and chest too far forward when stepping into kick push action.
2. Too much leg action—can cause overspin.
3. Failure to bring legs together when inverted.

BARANI (Fig. 212)

Figure 212

PT The barani is often confused with the cartwheel aerial. The movement is the same as a round-off without hands or the barani on the trampoline. Actually a quarter turn is made with the upper body on initial take off and a quarter turn after passing the vertical position. After the preparatory arm and leg lift, step forward on a bent right leg. Keeping head and chest up, immediately kick left leg upward while pushing with right. Eyes spot area on dismount mat; right shoulder rotates a quarter turn on takeoff; legs are brought together; then a quarter turn is initiated with right shoulder and hips. As legs pass head position, lift chest and focus eyes on end of beam. Land facing end of beam, arms obliquely forward and upward.

SP Same as for cartwheel aerial dismount.

CE 1. Lowering head and chest too far past knees during takeoff.
2. Allowing quarter turn to be made to the side of the body rather than directly in front.
3. Not bringing legs together in vertical position.
4. Allowing the legs to move around the vertical position rather than passing through it.

BACK SOMMIE DISMOUNT (Fig. 213)

Figure 213

PT Gain balance on balls of feet on end of beam with arms out to side of body. As knees and hips flex slightly, bring arms down, forward, and upward. Lean back very slightly to loose balance and forcefully spring off feet, bringing knees to chest. Head should remain in a normal position. A slight tilt of the head backward would be okay but, if the head is "thrown" back, the body will rotate downward rather than up and back. After back is parallel to ceiling, lift chest, extend hips and legs, and look for end of beam. Land with knees and hips slightly flexed and arms overhead or at the side.

SP Stand at end of the beam to the side of the performer. Place inside hand on back of upper thigh and outside hand on buttocks. Rotate with hands on thighs, and lift with hands on buttocks or lower back.

CE 1. Throwing head back.
2. Inadequate push from feet or lift with the arms.
3. Turning head to one side causing body to rotate on an angle rather than in a straight line.

VA *Back sommie in piked position.*

GAINER DISMOUNT (Fig. 214).

Figure 214

PT Stand approximately two feet from the end of the beam. Step forward on the right foot, immediately swing left leg forcefully forward and up, and push off of the beam with right foot to join left in tucked position. Arms come from side position to overhead; then they can touch knees in tuck position. Tilt head back only slightly. After the body has rotated in a three-quarter spin, extend hips and legs, and lift chest to come to stand.

SP Stand to side and end of beam. As push leg leaves beam, place near hand on back to help lift and far hand on hips to spin body.

CE 1. Inadequate kick push or arm lift.
      2. Not tucking tight enough (the tighter the tuck the faster the spin).
      3. Forcing the head back on takeoff. This only causes the body to drop.

Hint: Work gainer on trampoline or diving board before using beam.

Routine Composition for Class

Routines on the balance beam for classes should be short and easy but challenging and should contain all aspects of beam composition. The routine should contain a mount, locomotor skills, static positions, a tumbling skill, and a dismount. It is often not feasible to incorporate a tumbling skill in a class routine due to the level of ability of the students and the time factor for learning them well enough to perform.

For a beginning class it is best to have all students perform the same routine. If the students have had previous experience and training on the beam, they might enjoy creating their own routines.

There are many compulsory routines that could be used in a beginning class. Some may be found in the DGWS Gymnastic Guide, and the USGF Handbook.

SUGGESTED BEGINNING ROUTINE (for class) (Fig. 215)

Figure 215

Squat mount on left end of beam, quarter (90°) right with arms in second position. Single leg squat pose, stand, step left, step hop right, arms in second position. Step left; draw right foot to left; squat turn to right with arms obliquely backward. Forward roll (may omit) to straddle sitting position. Swing legs downbackward and upward to squat position on the beam with right foot in front of left. Stand, make half turn (180°) left on toes, and shift weight to right rear foot. Run left, run right, run left. Draw right foot to left, pose. Step forward on right foot chassé, half turn left on both feet (flat pivot) ending with left foot in front. Step right, slide left foot to right foot, changement, ending with left foot in front. Step left and kick right leg high while making quarter turn left. Arch jump dismount. (Make own arm movements.)

INTERMEDIATE ROUTINE (for class)

Step on mount. Pivot toe turn, squat jump, chassé, step tap leap, kick turn to lunge position. Forward roll to single leg squat, stand, two steps back, pose, step catwalk, step semisquat turn to pose. Run, run, leap, step, squat, then perform back shoulder roll to knee scale. Stand, quarter turn left, two slides sideways, quarter turn, grand battement, cartwheel dismount. (Make own arm movements.)

Routines for Competition

The time limit for competitive routines on the balance beam is from one minute fifteen to one minute thirty-five seconds. The watch starts as soon as the feet leave the mat or reuther board and stops when the dismount has been completed.

Movement on the beam should flow from one skill to the next with creative sequences. The routine should include locomotor skills, tumbling and acrobatic skills, turns, and static positions and must bring into action all parts of the body.

Static positions should be held only long enough to show control in that position.

There must be six elements of difficulty, two being of superior difficulty. For difficulty rating, refer to the FIG Code of Points Book.

A performer should vary the tempo (fast and slow) and the level (high, low, medium positions) of the skills in a routine to avoid monotony and to give an overall impression of lightness.

The performer should convey a feeling of confidence. Leaps should be as high as possible. Toe turns should not be performed flat footed. The entire beam routine should be lively and exciting to watch.

ROUTINES

1. Swing forward roll mount to single leg squat (legs very close), half turn in squat position, immediately execute squat jump. Stand, step into single leg pivot turn, grand battement forward, two cartwheels, step catwalk backwards, pose.

    Chainé, step, chassé, step back cancan kick, step kick turn to handstand forward roll to single leg squat. Quarter turn into full wolf turn to splits. Backward roll to squat position, body wave, one and one-half pirouette turn, back walkover, back walkover to lunge, step catwalk, step, split leap, step toe turn to arabesque. Step, front walkover, front walkover, front aerial dismount.

2. Handstand mount on end of beam into front walkover. Step pose, step split leap, jump turn, far arm cartwheel, step slide. Handstand forward roll, pirouette, two poses. English handstand, pirouette chest roll down to backward roll, pose. Stand, step tour jeté, step jazz turn, two back handsprings, back full twisting dismount.

3. Fig. 216.

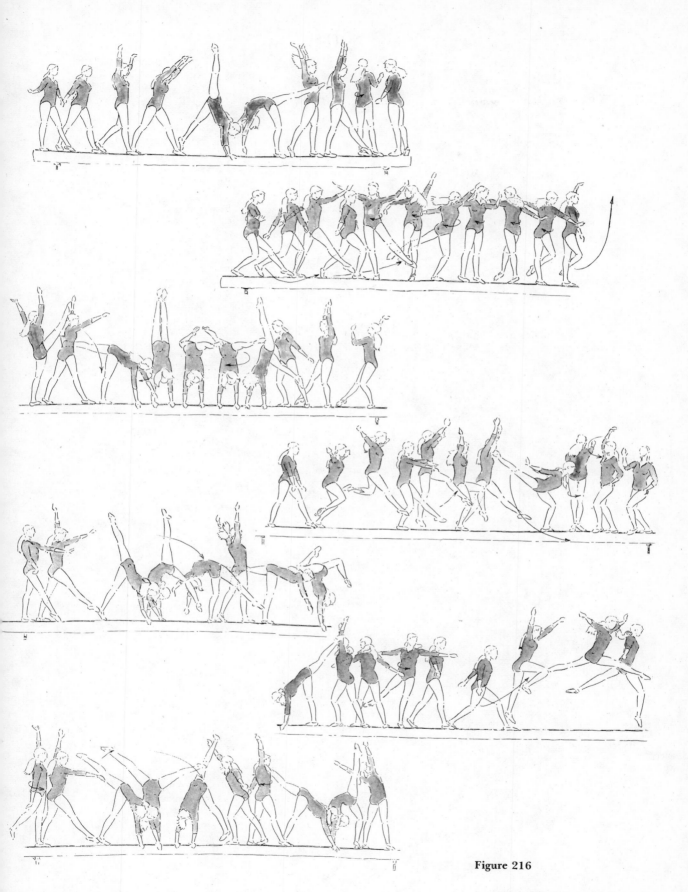

Figure 216

NOTES

CHAPTER FIVE
UNEVEN PARALLEL BARS

The uneven parallel bar event is most exciting to watch. As girls display their skill at releasing the low bar to grasp the high bar and then circle the low bar, there are many "ohs" and "ahs" from spectators.

To perform well in this spectacular event girls must first have interest, and of course we can't overlook the strength factor involved. If you can support or suspend your own body weight for at least ten seconds, you are on your way.

Skills will be described in the following classifications:

Mounts
Moves on one bar
Moves from one bar to the other
Releases
Dismounts

Note: Some of the releases (such as seat circle catch high bar) are described in the moves on one bar section as variations.

Since this event requires strength in the arms, shoulders, and abdominal and back areas, you must first strengthen those areas. The following exercises should be done daily.

Special Conditioning Exercises

PULL-UPS

Purpose: To develop strength in upper arm and shoulder.
Technique: Jump to long hang on high bar, ladder, or some other object to hang from. Grasp with

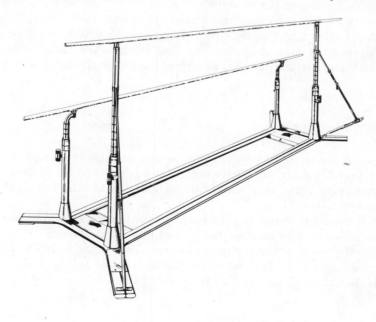

forward grip (palms forward). Keeping body as straight as possible, bend arms and pull body upward until chin reaches over top of bar.

Variation: Chin-up. Same technique with hands in reverse grip.

Hint: Have partner assist until pull-up can be done alone. Stand close to performer, grasp above knee, and use your legs to assist in lifting so as not to strain back.

LEG LIFTS

Purpose: To develop rectus abdominus and quadreceps. Also acts as isometric exercise for the upper arms and grip.

Technique: Hang from wall ladder or high bar; lift toes slowly to head (or to "L" position), then slowly lower them to starting position. Work up to ten.

SIT-UPS WITH TWIST

Purpose: To develop abdominal and lower back muscles.

Technique: Assume supine position with legs straight and together, hands on shoulders; tilt pelvis and *curl* up to an erect sitting position. Twist to right and touch left elbow to right knee. Return to original position and repeat to other side. Work up to at least fifteen.

SWAN EXERCISE

Purpose: To develop flexibility in upper abdomen and lower back. Assists in tightening gluteal muscles and strengthening lower back.

Technique: From prone position, arms overhead:
1. Lift arms, tilt head back, tense gluteal muscles, and arch back as far back and up as possible.
2. Keep upper body on floor, tense gluteal muscles, lift legs with heels together (legs straight) as far off the floor as possible.
3. Combine 1 and 2 simultaneously.

Variation: Have partner lift arms then legs. (This is for flexibility.)
1. Straddle body around chest area; grasp arms above elbows and lift body as far as possible, making sure hips do not leave the floor.
2. Sit on performer's buttocks and grasp legs above knee and lift legs as high as possible.

SHOULDER STRETCH —partner exericse

Purpose: To develop flexibility in the shoulder area.

Technique: Sit on floor with legs together and straight and with back erect. Partner stands behind and places leg (not knee) against performer's back. Reach between arms, grasp above elbows, force arms and shoulders up and back while simultaneously forcing chest forward with leg. Switch partners and repeat. Stretch shoulder area a little further each time.

Safety Hints

1. Check bars before each use to make sure they are secure in their supports.
2. Surround bars with mats, making sure that enough area is covered for mounts and dismounts.
3. If bars have a tendency to rock, they should be weighted with sand bags, other members of the class, or by some other method.
4. If a reuther board is used for mounting the bars, it should be removed as soon as the performer is on the bars and will not be hindered by the person moving the board.
5. Use chalk and/or hand grips to prevent palms of hands from being ripped.
6. Do not continue working on the bars when the hands feel hot and become red because that is a sign that the hands should be given a rest so they won't rip.

7. Do not allow students on the bars unsupervised.
8. Have a definite skill progression for each class.

Grips

FORWARD (over) (Fig. 217)

The forward or over grip is used for approximately 75 percent of all uneven parallel bar skills. The hands are placed on the bars with the back of the hand (knuckles) facing upward. The thumb may be either alongside the fingers or around the bar. This is a matter of preference since the size of individuals hands vary.

Figure 217

REVERSE (under) (Fig. 218)

The reverse or under grip has the hands on the bar with the fingers facing upward and the thumb around the bar.

Figure 218

MIXED GRIP (Fig. 219)

One hand in the forward grip and the other hand in a reversed grip.

Figure 219

EAGLE GRIP (twist grip) (Fig. 220)

This grip is used for just a few skills. The arms are lifted sideways and grasp the bar with backs of hands facing up and thumbs under bar.

Figure 220

Skills

In all skills it will be assumed that knees are straight and toes are pointed unless otherwise stated.

MOUNTS

JUMP TO FRONT SUPPORT (Fig. 221)

Figure 221

PT   Stand between bars, close to and facing low bar. Grasp low bar with forward grip. Bend knees and spring vertically; extend arms and allow upper thighs to come to rest on the low bar. Keep head up, legs together and straight, slight arch in back. Keep shoulders forward of the bar.

SP   Assist weak girls by lifting at waist.

CE   1. Failure to keep elbows straight (locked) when support position is achieved.
      2. Failure to keep body taut and slightly arched.
      3. Allowing shoulders to be shrugged (failure to extend in shoulders and keep head up).

MO   1. Single leg flank to stride support.
      2. Back hip circle.
      3. Front hip circle.
      4. Single or double leg shoot through.
      5. Squat stand.
      6. Straddle stand.
      7. Double leg shoot through.
      8. Stoop stand.
      9. Underswing dismount.
     10. Drop kip.
     11. Free straddle support.

*BACK HIP PULLOVER TO
FRONT SUPPORT ON LOW BAR*
(Fig. 222)

Figure 222

PT   Stand between bars facing low bar; grasp bar with forward grip with body close to bar and elbows bent. Keep one foot slightly in front of the other with weight on back foot. Shift weight to forward foot and simultaneously swing back leg forward and upward to lift hips to the bar. As hips move under the bar, push off with forward foot and allow legs to come together as body is revolving around the bars. Keep elbows bent and pull hips to the bar. Rotate grip backward to allow wrists to finish over hands to help maintain support on hands. Finish in front support by lifting head and extending arms as the pullover is completed.

SP Stand beside performer outside low bar. Place inside hand on small of back and outside hand on back of upper thighs. Help keep hips close to bar by lifting legs if necessary.

CE . 1. Allowing arms to extend (straighten). When this happens, the hips cannot be kept close to the bar and the performer's lower body will drop to the mat.
   2. Failure to kick or swing vigorously with the back leg and push off with the forward foot.
   3. Failure to rotate hand grip backward.
   4. Failure to end in front support.

MO Same as for jump to front support.

BEAT SWING SQUAT OVER (from long hang on high bar) (Fig. 223a)

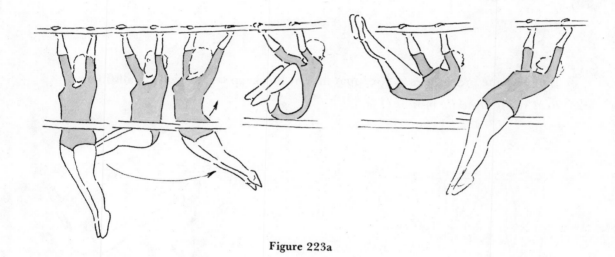

Figure 223a

PT Jump to long hang on high bar facing the low bar. Use forward grip. Keeping upper body as motionless as possible, force hips backward and lift legs forward and up, then hips forward and legs back. As hips start to move forward draw knees to chest and extend legs upward. As body moves forward, force hips upward (extend hips) and lower backs of upper thighs to the low bar. Extend upper body to finish in rear support.

SP Stand beside performer between bars. Place hands on waist to help keep upper body motionless. Then pull waist (and hips) back slightly as squat movement is initiated.

CE 1. Improper timing on swing.
   2. Failure to lift knees to chest at start of second forward swing of legs.
   3. Failure to lower backs of upper thigh onto bar with control.
   4. Failure to make beat swing short and forceful.

MO 1. Stem rise to high bar.
   2. Pull over to high bar.
   3. Kip to high bar.
   4. Release high bar, grasp lower bar, and perform front or back seat circle.

VA   1. *Beat swing stoop over mount* (Fig. 223b)

Figure 223b

Follow same procedures as for squat mount but keep legs straight at all times.

2. *Beat swing straddle mount* (Fig. 224)

Figure 224

Follow same procedures as for squat mount but lift legs upward and sideward in a wide straddle before placing backs of upper thighs on the bar; then finish in a rear seat support with hands on high bar.

BACK HIP CIRCLE MOUNT (using reuther board) (Fig. 225)

Figure 225

PT After a two-foot takeoff on reuther board, grasp low bar and allow shoulders to go forward keeping arms straight. Extend body completely to reach a horizontal position. Shoulders are slightly forward of low bar toward high bar. Bring body to bar. When hips contact bar, flex hips and continue with back hip circle.

SP In the beginning the spotter can assist at the abdomen and upper thigh area by lifting person to horizontal position. The back hip circle portion should be spotted like a regular back hip circle.

CE 1. Not allowing shoulders to be over hand position.
2. Not hitting horizontal position with body completely tight.
3. Flexing at the hips before contacting bar.

MO Anything that can be done from a front support position.

VA Free back hip circle mount.

GLIDE KIP MOUNT (Fig. 226)

Figure 226

PT Stand under high bar facing low bar or stand in front of low bar facing toward low and high bars. To learn, start with hands in forward grip on bar (eventually stand about three feet behind bar) and jump to bar. The jump into the glide gives the performer more momentum and more time to bring her feet to the bar before the kip.

Arms extended and shoulders relaxed, jump up and forward, lifting the hips backupward. Lift the legs upward so that they will be a few inches above the mat. Keep arms and shoulders extended and allow body to glide under the bar to an extended position. As full body extension is achieved, *immediately* flex hips, lifting ankles to the bar. As body begins backward swinging motion in pike position, force legs *up* along the bar by partially extending hips and forcefully pushing downward with extended arms. As hips reach bar level, the legs continue moving outdownward. The hips at this point extend further. The pushing-down action from the extended arms must be followed through until the performer finishes in a front support position with the arms and shoulders fully extended and chin up. Just before completing the skill, rotate grip slightly forward.

SP Two spotters, one on each side of performer in front of bar. Reach under bar and place inside hand on lower back and outside hand on back of upper thighs (help keep hips close to bar). Inside hand helps performer get to front support position after kipping movement of legs and hips is initiated.

CE 1. Failure to thrust hips back and up on jump to bar.
2. Failure to keep arms and shoulders extended on glide.
3. Keeping legs too high on glide.
4. Failure to extend body at end of glide.
5. Failure to forcefully lift legs to bar as soon as glide is completed and to keep hips from dropping backward.
6. Failure to force legs upward until hips reach bar (many beginners have the tendency to kip down and out rather than up and out).
7. Failure to keep arms straight and to push down on the bar to reach the front support position.

MO Same as for front support plus variations on following page.

VA 1. *Glide with legs in straddle position* (Fig. 227)

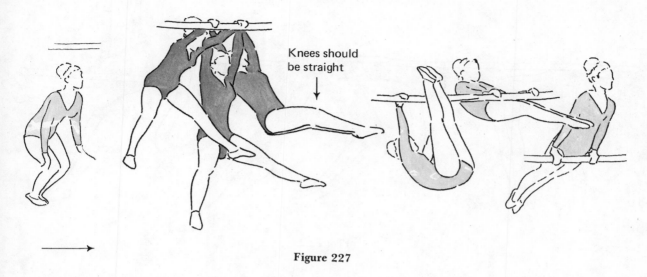

Knees should be straight

Figure 227

2. *Glide, single leg shoot through to stride position* (Fig. 228)

Figure 228

PT Follow same procedures as for kip, but when body has reached extended position in glide, force one leg between hands so that it can continue over the bar. Keep legs free of the bar and finish in a wide stride position.

CE 1. Not forcing leg through arms while hips are forward.
2. Not extending hips as body is ready to pass over bar to final position.

3. *Glide Kip—Catch high bar* (Fig. 229)

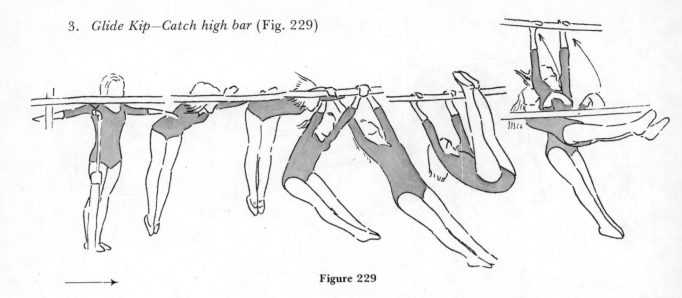

Figure 229

PT Same procedures as for regular kip. As most of kip is completed (hips to bar), reach for the high bar. Look at the high bar as the initial kipping action is started.

SP Stand between bars. As feet are brought to bar, place outside hand on small of back to prevent a fall and inside hand under the bar on the back of the thighs. Maintain contact and help lift the performer to the high bar, making sure she has a firm grip on it.

CE 1. Failure to complete at least half the kip on the low bar before quickly catching the high bar.
2. Failure to look at high bar when catching it.

4. *Glide to double leg shoot through to rear support* (Fig. 230)

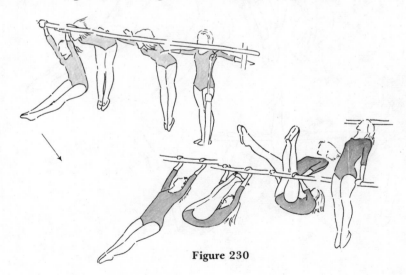

Figure 230

PT Same procedures as on a regular glide to the extended position. As this position is reached, force both legs between hands. Allow body to ride under the low bar in a piked position until the backs of the upper thighs are under the bar. Then forcefully pull with the hands, maintain the pike, and pass through an L support position to a rear support on the low bar. As the body moves over the top of the low bar, rotate grip forward and lift head and chest.

SP Same as for regular kip but assist at shoulders while inverted in pike position throughout entire skill.

CE 1. Not forcing legs through arms while hips are forward on the glide position.
2. Failure to maintain pike.
3. Failure to rotate grip when coming over top of bar.

5. *Back kip (reverse kip)* (Fig. 231)

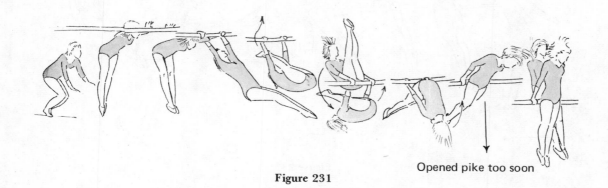

Opened pike too soon

Figure 231

PT The back kip is a combination of the glide double leg shoot through (third variation of the kip) and a back seat circle.

SWITCH GLIDE KIP (straddle position) (Fig. 232)

Hand change

Figure 232

PT From a straddle glide keep hips slightly flexed, rotate hips and shoulders, and turn head to right while releasing right hand. Regrasp bar, trying not to let hips ride forward. Quickly change grip of left hand to a forward grip, and continue into the second glide. Bring ankles to bar and finish kip. (Some girls prefer to finish with a mixed grip rather than make the second change during the kip).

SP Same as for a regular kip. You may assist at the waist on the turn if necessary.

CE 1. Inadequate first glide.
2. Allowing hips to ride forward toward bar on turn.
3. Poor timing in hand switch and kip.

FRONT HIP CIRCLE (done with reuther board) (Fig. 233)

Figure 233

PT Approaching with a run and hurdle from the board, spring vertically (momentum will carry the body forward) and contact the low bar on upper thighs with body completely stretched, arms overhead, and head up. Maintain this position momentarily, then allow the upper body to initiate the forward movement. Just before the body reaches the inverted position, pike sharply, grasp the bar with a forward grip. As the body continues moving around the bar, extend the arms fully, keep head and chest up, and finish in a front support.

SP Two spotters, one at each side standing in front of the low bar between the reuther board and bar. Allow just enough room for the performer to pass through. As performer leaves the board, each spotter grasps a leg above the knee to make sure that she contacts the bar on upper thighs. After hip circle is started, reach hand under bar and place inside hand on hips and outside hand on the back to keep hips close to the bar.

CE 1. Failure to contact body in proper position on thighs, with body completely arched and head up.
2. Failure to pause momentarily, then begin forward movement with upper body.
3. Piking too soon or too late during hip circle.
4. Failure to grasp bar, extend arms, and rotate grip forward to top of bar and to finish in a front support with head and chest up.

MO 1. All those skills listed from the front support mount.
2. Cast back to squat stand, grasp high bar, underswing half turn to hip circle on low bar.
3. Cast back to squat stand, grasp high bar, sole circle half turn to hip circle on low bar (refer to page 158 for details of sole circle).

VA Perform double front hip circle grasping legs below knee while rotating around the bar one and three-quarters times; then grasp bar and finish in front support as for front hip circle mount.

Hint: When rotating, keep arms bent and forearms close to the bar in order to keep body close to the bar. Then straighten the arms forcefully as hands are placed on the bar to push body to a front support position.

Figure 234

PT Using reuther board, jump vertically over the low bar, driving knees to chest, forcefully push with hands on releasing the low bar, and grasp the high bar with a forward grip. As the hips clear the low bar, forcefully extend body (emphasizing hip extension) and, just as hips reach the fully extended position, release right hand, turning hips and shoulders 180°. Regrasp the bar with right hand. At this point of the skill, body should be fully extended behind hands, which are in a mixed grip (left hand undergrip, right hand overgrip). The left hand does not release the high bar.

SP Two spotters, one standing in front of low bar and one standing between bars. The spotter in front of the bar helps performer clear the low bar by lifting her hips. The spotter between the bars places her inside hand on the small of the back and outside hand on the thighs until the performer grasps the high bar and has fully extended. This spotter may also assist with the turn.

CE 1. Insufficient spring from the board.
      2. Insufficient push with hands from the low bar.
      3. Stopping movement when making contact with the high bar.
      4. Not fully extending hips on the underswing.
      5. Turning too soon or too late from the extension.

MO 1. Hip circle on low bar.
      2. Drop to low bar, then kip.
      3. Hip circle on low bar to eagle catch.

STRADDLE OVER, STRADDLE BACK (Fig. 235)

Figure 235

PT From takeoff on reuther board, push forcefully down on the low bar as hips thrust backupward and legs lift in a wide high straddle. Immediately reach for the high bar and go into a forceful long hang, forcing hips forward and heels backward. After momentary hesitation, bend arms slightly and pull on high bar as hips are forced backward. Lift heels up, forcing a wide straddle as body moves backward over low bar. Regrasp low bar, keeping hips back for a nice glide kip.

SP This skill is difficult to spot since legs are in a straddle position. Stand in front of low bar ready to step in after performer leaves board. Depending on size of spotter and performer, grasp waist and lift up and forward over low bar, *or* place hands on back and upper thighs and lift up and over. On return straddle over the bar, grasp waist area again and assist in lifting up and back over low bar.

CE 1. Inadequate punch off board, straddle of legs, or push from low bar with hands.
2. Failure to hit a taut long-hang position.
3. Staying in long-hang position too long (causing loss of momentum).
4. Insufficient pull of arms and leg lift to straddle on return over low bar.
5. Failure to keep hips back so slide kip can be completed.

MO Anything that can be done from a front support position.

VA Straddle or squat over and immediate kip to high bar from long hang.

HANDSTAND MOUNT ON LOW BAR (Fig. 236)

Figure 236

PT   After takeoff on reuther board, grasp low bar. Keeping head up and back and arms straight, flex hips and stay in piked straddle position until hips are over hands. At this point lift legs together to a completely extended handstand position. (The board has to be punched as if going to vault to get enough lift).

SP   1. One spotter stands in front of low bar, careful not to impede gymnast, and lifts at hip area. Other spotter stands on low bar, with leg over high bar for support, and grabs upper thigh when going into handstand position.

      2. Stand between bars slightly to side of performer. Grasp waist area as piked straddle is achieved. Help lift hips and legs up into handstand position.

CE   1. Insufficient punch off board.

      2. Not getting hips over hands before going into handstand and not keeping arms straight.

MO 1. To rear seat support on high bar, then front or back seat circle.

      2. Do not allow body to touch high bar—just hit handstand position then drop to hip circle on low bar.

      3. Straddle legs down to sole circle on low bar.

MOVES ON ONE BAR

All the following skills should be mastered on the low bar before transfering to the high bar. If there are no uneven parallel bars available, these skills can be learned on a horizontal bar lowered to the height of the uneven low bar, or one bar from a set of even parallel bars can be removed.

SWAN BALANCE (Fig. 237)

PT From a front support position, balance body on upper thigh area and lift arms overhead. (Every individual's exact balance point is different, so you must experiment to find yours.)

SP Stand between bars and control the performer's balance by holding ankles, or stand in front of the bar and spot shoulder area to keep upper body from falling forward.

MO 1. Go back to front support position; hands regrasp bar in forward grip; perform any of the skills listed from the front support position.
2. Front hip circle.

Figure 237

SINGLE LEG FLANK TO A STRIDE LEG SUPPORT (Fig. 238)

Figure 238

PT From a front support position with a forward grip, lift left leg upward and sideways over the low bar. Remove left hand, allow leg to pass over, replace hand on the bar, and immediately hold a stride leg support. Weight is on hands, the rest of the body is completely free of the bar. When lifting left hand off the bar, shift weight to right hand. Right arm must remain locked (straight) at all times. The movement, once learned, should be a fast one.

SP 1. Stand in front of performer, grasp upper arm or elbow of right arm, and help keep arm straight until skill is completed.
2. Stand between bars. Hold ankle that will not be flanking and wrist of hand that will not be leaving bar.

CE 1. Failure to keep shoulders slightly forward of bar until stride position is attained.
2. Failure to keep right arm straight at all times.
3. Failure to lift left leg high enough to clear bar.
4. Failure to keep legs straight.

MO 1. Single leg swing down and up.
2. Single leg flank dismount with quarter turn.
3. Mill circle.
4. Mill circle catch high bar.

CAST (push away and return to bar) (Fig. 239)

Figure 239

PT From front support position with hands in a forward grip, flex hips, bringing legs under bar (allow arms to slightly flex) and move shoulders forward of the bar. Thrust legs backupward, forcing body (except hands) away from the bar, and extend arms. Return to the bar in a fully extended (arched) position.

Hint: Try to swing legs high enough to have calves make contact with the high bar.

SP Stand between bars. Inside hand reaches under the bar and is placed behind elbow (palm against elbow) to force the shoulders forward. Place the outside hand on the upper thigh to help lift body away from the bar.

CE 1. Allowing arms to bend after hips leave the bar.
2. Not keeping head up and shoulders forward of the bar.
3. Insufficient thrust of legs.
4. Allowing legs to bend.
5. Not returning to the bar in an arched position.

MO 1. Back hip circle.
2. This movement is also used for the following skills, but body does not return to the bar in an arched position before continuing with the skills.
    a. Single leg shoot through to stride support.
    b. Double leg shoot through to rear support.
    c. Squat stand.
    d. Straddle stand.
    e. Stoop stand.
    f. Squat over dismount.

SINGLE LEG SHOOT THROUGH (Fig. 240)

Figure 240

PT From a front support with a forward grip, cast away from the bar, keeping arms straight and shoulders forward of the bar. As the body is suspended away from the bar, forcefully lift hips and bring one knee to chest; then extend it forward over the low bar as body is returning to the bar. Finish in a stride position with entire body weight on hands.

SP Two spotters, one in front of the low bar, one between the bars. The spotter between the bars stands on the nonbending leg side. Grasp leg above knee with inside hand and ankle with outside hand, and help keep body suspended by lifting leg until the other knee is bent and extended over the bar. The spotter in front of the bar supports upper arms to make sure shoulders remain forward of the bar at all times and to prevent performer from collapsing.

CE 1. Insufficient cast.
   2. Failure to keep shoulders forward of the bar.
   3. Allowing arms to bend.
   4. Failure to bend knee to chest and to extend it over the bar in one rapid movement.
   5. Allowing knee to be turned out rather than bringing it directly to the chest.

MO 1. Mill circle.
   2. Mill circle catch the high bar.
   3. Single leg flank dismount with quarter turn.

BACK HIP CIRCLE (Fig. 241)

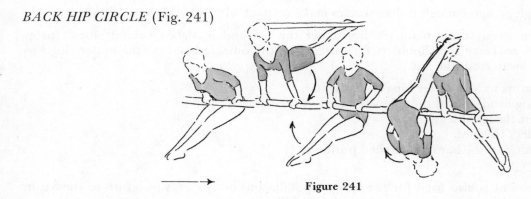

Figure 241

PT From a front support position with the hands in a forward grip, cast away from the bar and return in an straight body position, contacting the bar at the lower abdominal area. As soon as the body contacts the bar, flex hips and force legs forward. Bend arms slightly to keep hips close to the bar and rotate around the bar at hip area. As soon as the body has completed three-quarters of the circle, rotate hands (grip) around the bar and extend arms to finish in a front support position.

SP Stand in front of the bar. Reach under the bar and place inside hand on back as body returns to the bar from the cast and outside hand on back of upper thigh to help rotate and keep hips close to the bar. After hips have circled bar, slide outside hand up to arm to help maintain front support position.

CE 1. Poor cast.
2. Failure to pike as hips contact the bar (many beginners pike too soon).
3. Failure to slightly bend arms and continually pull hips to the bar.
4. Failure to keep legs straight at all times.
5. Failure to rotate hands (grip) around the bar, fully extend arms and shoulders, and open body to finish in a front support position.

MO Any skill from the front support position.

SINGLE LEG SWING DOWN AND UP (Fig. 242)

Figure 242

Note: This particular skill is not one that you will find in a competitive routine. It is merely a lead-up skill for other moves.

PT From a stride support, right leg in front, hands in a forward grip, shift hips backward, bending right leg so that knee hooks over the bar, and swing back and down under the bar. As momentum under the bar stops, swing left leg down and back upward forcefully; push against the bar with hands and return to the stride position. Just as thigh of right leg moves over the bar, slightly bend elbows, rotate hands to the top of the bar, and extend arms, right leg and upper body to finish in a stride position.

SP Stand between bars to left of performer. As body swings under bar, place outside hand on back to prevent a fall, and as body starts upward motion, reach under the bar and place inside hand on upper thigh to assist with the pumping action of the left leg.

CE 1. Allowing arms to bend and body to curl forward on the back swing.
2. Not using left (pumping leg) forcefully.
3. Failure to rotate grip as body returns to the stride support position.
4. Failure to extend right leg and upper body as body reaches the stride position.

MILL CIRCLE (Fig. 243)

PT   From a stride support (right leg forward) using the reverse grip, lift body up from the bars and support weight on hands. Keep chest and head up; arch back slightly. Shift weight forward by leading with right foot as if to step forward and extend hips. This movement should force most of the body weight over the bar and allow body to rotate around the bar. For added momentum, lift back leg so that legs are in a wide split position. Keep legs apart and body straight throughout skill. As upper body is coming to the original position, rotate hand forward around the bar, forcing wrist forward, lifting upper body (slightly arching the back to stop momentum), and finish in a stride support.

Note: To learn, it sometimes helps to bring legs together while in the inverted position; however, you must keep weight on hands and legs *off of* bars.

Figure 243

SP   Stand between bars, reach under the bar with inside hand, and grasp elbow or wrist with palm to help keep performer's arms straight and to force body around the bar by pushing forward and then upward as the performer comes to the original position. Outside hand supports the back during the last quarter of the skill. A second spotter can reach under the bar and place inside hand on back of thigh to push leg forward at the start of the skill.

CE   1.   Failure to lift body off the bar and support weight with hands before starting forward motion.
2.   Failure to step out to allow hips to pass forward of the bar and to develop momentum.
3.   Not keeping head and chest up throughout skill (chin should drop a bit just before finishing the skill).
4.   Allowing upper body to curl when rotating.
5.   Bending arms and legs during skill.
6.   Not moving hands around bar with body and not forcing them forward during the last quarter of the skill.

MO   1.   Single leg flank to rear support position; then grasp high bar and move to high bar by performing a stem rise, pullover, or kip.
2.   Single leg flank dismount with quarter turn.
3.   Single leg flank with half turn to front support facing high bar.

VA 1. *Mill circle, catch high bar* (Fig. 244)

Hands must grasp simultaneously

Figure 244

PT Same procedures as for the beginning of the mill circle. When body is inverted under the bar, begin looking for high bar and, when body has almost reached the original position, reach for the high bar, keeping the body straight (hips forward).

SP Stand between bars. As soon as the performer has passed the inverted position, place inside hand on lower back and outside hand on upper back, and help performer to the high bar. Maintain contact until grasp has been made on high bar.

CE 1. Poor mill circle.
2. Failure to keep eyes open and look for the high bar.
3. Reaching for the bar too soon, or with one hand at a time.
4. Failure to keep hips moving forward throughout entire skill.

MO 1. Single or double leg stem rise.
2. Pullover from low to high.
3. Kip from low to high bar.

FRONT HIP CIRCLE (Fig. 245)

Figure 245

PT Assume front support position with the hands in a forward grip and body resting high on upper thighs; keep head up and lean forward, leading with chest and keeping entire body extended. Just before body reaches the inverted position, flex (pike) upper body, bend elbows slightly, and continue rotating around the bar. Push down forcefully on the bar with hands, and just before body returns to the original position, forcefully rotate hands forward, extend arms and shoulders, and finish in a front support.

SP   Two spotters between bars. Reach under the bar with inside hand and spot lower back and hip area. As body passes the inverted position, place outside hand on back. (Transfer inside hand to legs to control forward movement, if necessary.)

CE   1.   Not starting with thighs high enough on the bar (insufficient extension of shoulders and arms).
2.   Failure to keep head and chest up, to extend shoulders, and to arch back.
3.   Piking too soon or too late.
4.   Failure to keep hips in contact with the bar throughout skill.
5.   Failure to extend arms and shoulders upon returning to original position.

MO   Any skill from the front support position.

VA   1.   *Free front hip circle (starting with hands over head)* (Fig. 246)

Figure 246

PT   Front support, body high on bar, arms overhead. Forcefully swing arms down, backward, and upward as body follows in a fully arched position. Just before reaching the inverted position, pike upper body and grasp the bar in a forward grip; continue movement to front support as for hip circle.

2.   *Front hip circle, catch high bar* (Fig. 247)

Figure 247

SQUAT STAND (Fig. 248)

Figure 248

PT From a front support with hands in a forward grip, push away (cast) from the bar forcefully. While body is extended and suspended, lift hips and bring knees to chest; then place toes on bar between hands. Lift head and chest, grip the bar tightly, and *keep hips low to maintain balance*.

SP One spotter between bars, other spotter in front of bar. The spotter standing between the bars reaches over the bar with inside hand to support upper arm and keep shoulders forward of the bar. Place outside hand on back of thigh (palm up) to help lift as performer squats to bar. Spotter in front of bar supports upper arm to keep shoulders forward of bar.

CE
1. Poor cast.
2. Insufficient height on cast to allow knees to be brought to the chest.
3. Slow leg action in cast, to squat, or both.
4. Not keeping shoulders forward of the bar.
5. Failure to lower hips and to keep head and chest up as feet contact bar.

MO
1. Stand, half turn (180°), front support on high bar, back hip circle.
2. Stand, reach back grasp high bar, dislocate.
3. Stand, reach back grasp high bar, back straddle catch.
4. Stand, grasp high bar, 180° turn, sole circle, underswing with half turn.
5. Stand, reach back grasp high bar, jump to L support, drop back flank cut catch or drop back flank dismount (or straddle cut catch or dismount).
6. Stand, reach back grasp high bar, jump to L support, front or back seat circle.

DOUBLE LEG SHOOT THROUGH (Fig. 249)

PT From a front support with a forward grip, cast forcefully, bend both legs, drawing knees to chest, and immediately extend legs forward over low bar. Keep arms straight throughout skill and squeeze bar with hands. Finish in an L support or rear support with weight supported on hands.

SP Two spotters. One in front of the low bar holding upper arm to keep shoulders forward of the bar. The other spotter between the bars with inside hand over or under bar (depending on height of spotter) grasping elbow to help keep shoulders forward and outside hand under back of upper thigh to help performer squat over bar to support position.

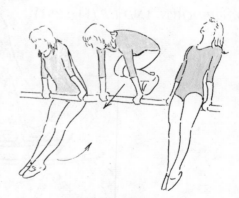

Figure 249

CE
1. Poor cast.
2. Slow leg action on drawing knees to chest and extending them forward over the bar.
3. Not keeping shoulders forward of the bar.
4. Allowing toes to contact the bar when shooting through.
5. Failure to hold the L support.

MO 1. When performed on low bar:
    a. Drop back and up to L support.
    b. Drop back and up and catch the high bar.
    c. Back seat circle.
    d. Change hands to reverse grip and perform forward seat circle.
    e. Dislocate to glide kip catch.
  2. When performed on the high bar:
    a. Back seat circle.
    b. Change hands to reverse grip and perform front seat circle or dislocate.
    c. Drop back flank cut catch or flank cut dismount.
    d. Drop back straddle cut catch or straddle cut dismount.
    e. Drop back (perform three-quarters of back seat circle; then drop to glide kip on low bar).

CAST FREE STRADDLE SUPPORT (Fig. 250)

Figure 250

PT Same procedures as for double leg shoot through except that the legs are forcefully raised to the side and then forward over the bar to the outside of the hands and remain completely free of the bar. Support on hands only. Hips must be raised forcefully then lowered as the straddle position is achieved.

SP One spotter stands in front of the bars to support upper arms and to keep shoulders forward of the bar. A second spotter can stand between bars behind performer and, as she straddles, places hands on back of upper thighs and assists her in clearing the bar.

MO 1. On low bar: underswing, half turn to glide kip to front support, or double leg shoot through.
  2. On high bar: underswing, half turn and hip circle on low bar.

DROP DOWN AND UP (Fig. 251)

Figure 251

PT This very basic skill should always be taught, as it teaches timing and control in the piked position; it is also the beginning, middle, or end of several skills. Start in a rear seat support with hands in a forward grip. Lift body off bar while lifting ankles to face. With arms completely straight, drop back and under the bar, keeping hips fairly close to the bar. As soon as the momentum stops, forward motion will begin. At this point push down on the bar forcefully, remain in the tight pike, and move grip slightly forward as body moves back to starting position. Hips will extend at this point to finish in a rear sitting position.

SP Stand to the side of the performer between bars. Place inside hand on buttocks and outside hand on back. Go with the movement, and assist by pushing on back during latter part of return movement.

CE 1. Bending arms at any time during skill.
2. Allowing upper body to go forward in the beginning rather than lifting legs to upper body.
3. Trying to return to rear sitting position too soon rather than taking full advantage of the swinging action.

VA 1. Drop down and, on return, catch high bar.

FRONT SEAT CIRCLE (Fig. 252)

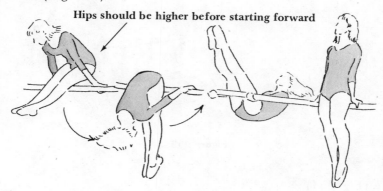

Hips should be higher before starting forward

Figure 252

PT From L support with reverse grip; lift hips back and *up* so the body is in a tight pike and the lower part of the leg is close to (but not touching) the bar. Lean forward, keeping arms straight and body in tight pike, and rotate around the bar allowing the hands to rotate also. The body rotates without legs or thighs touching the bar. Look at knees during skill. As the body passes the inverted position under the bar and is approaching the original position, rotate the hands forward (thumbs leading) and slightly raise the shoulders and forcefully extend the arms to finish in the original position. Tilt head up; eyes spot stationary object at eye level.

SP Two spotters stand between bars. Reach under bar and grasp elbow or wrist with inside hand. Force body forward. As body comes under bar, place far arm on back to assist in lifting to original position.

CE 1. Failure to keep body free of bar throughout skill.
2. Failure to lift hips as high as possible before beginning forward movement.
3. Failure to remain in a piked position throughout skill; opening up only slightly upon returning to original position.
4. Failure to keep arms perfectly straight, especially at the beginning of the skill.
5. Failure to rotate hands around bar and then rotate thumb and wrist forward during the last quarter of the skill.

MO 1. On low bar:
    a. Change hands to reverse grip, back seat circle.
    b. Sit, grasp high bar, kip to high bar.
    c. Sit, grasp high bar, kip to double leg shoot through, drop back, drop kip on low bar.
  2. On high bar:
    a. Dislocate, hip circle low bar.
    b. Change the hands to a forward grip, back seat circle.
    c. Change the hands to a forward grip, drop back flank cut catch or dismount.
    d. Change the hands to a forward grip, drop back straddle cut catch or dismount.

VA   *Front seat circle, catch high bar* (Fig. 253)

PT   As soon as the body passes the inverted position, open the tight pike position, extend hips, and reach for the high bar.

SP   Same as for mill circle catch.

Figure 253

BACK SEAT CIRCLE (Fig. 254)

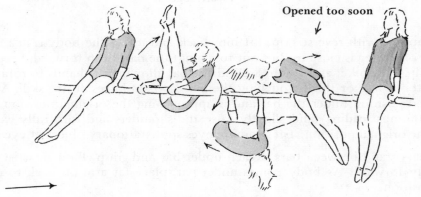

Figure 254

PT   From an L position with the hands in a forward grip, force knees to head so that body forms a tight pike with hips over bar. Shift weight backward and continue rotating around the bar in a tight pike. Move hands around the bar with rest of body; just as body is three-quarters way around, rotate hands forcefully forward, lift head and spot object at eye level (over the bar), and finish in the original position.

SP Stand in front of the low bar. Reach under the bar with inside hand and grasp performer's upper arm. As the performer rotates, place outside hand on upper leg to help keep hips away from bar and body in tight pike.

CE 1. Failure to keep body (except hands) free of bar throughout skill.
2. Failure to go into deep pike and remain in this position throughout the skill.
3. Failure to keep arms perfectly straight, especially on the drop backward.
4. Opening pike before returning to L position.
5. Failure to rotate hands around the bar.

MO Same as for front seat circle.

MOVES FROM ONE BAR TO THE OTHER

PULLOVER FROM LOW BAR TO HIGH BAR (Fig. 255)

Figure 255

PT Grasp high bar with forward grip. Place right foot on low bar with right knee forward of right foot. Extend left leg over the low bar. Lower left leg, then forcefully swing leg up over the high bar while simultaneously bending arms (pulling) to help get hips to the high bar. Immediately push with right foot; bring legs together as body rotates. Lift head and chest; rotate grip and extend arms to finish in a front support on the high bar.

SP Stand between bars and assist by pushing hips to the high bar. As the performer reaches the support position, grasp ankles to assist with balance.

CE 1. Failure to swing straight leg forcefully up and back over bar.
2. Failure to pull with arms and push with foot against low bar.
3. Failure to rotate grip and extend arms, then lift head to finish in a front support.

MO 1. Any skill listed from a front support position.
2. Cast to a long hang and any move from that position.

DOUBLE LEG STEM RISE (Fig. 256)

Notice good grip movement forward at this point

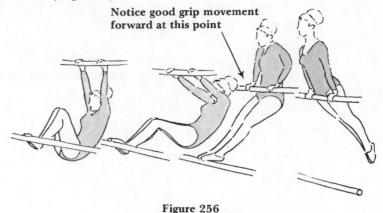

Figure 256

PT 1. Grasp high bar with forward grip; place both feet (toes) on low bar. Extend legs, forcing hips to high bar by forcefully pushing downward on the high bar. Allow elbows to bend slightly to let shoulders pass over bar. Feet remain on the low bar until the body is almost to a front support position. Rotate grip, extend arms and shoulders and finish in a front support.

Note: The timing or coordination of the leg extension and arm pull is very important on both the single and double stem rise. The hips must move backward, then upward as if moving around a large semicircle.

2. Start in L position (toes on low bar). Keep legs straight at all times. Pull up *slightly* with arms while pushing against low bar. Lower body to original L; then forcefully pull with hands and push against bar with feet until in a front support position.

SP Stand under high bar. Place outside hand on hip, inside hand on back of upper thigh; assist in backward, then upward movement.

CE 1. Failure to extend legs backward as body is being pulled to the bar by the arms.
2. Not allowing shoulders to pass over bar.
3. Allowing feet to leave low bar before body is ready to extend to front support position.
4. Failure to rotate grip, extend arms, and lift head and chest to end in a front support.

MO 1. Any skill from a front support position on the low bar.
2. Underswing to stride support.
3. Cast to long hang.
4. Underswing dismount over low bar.
5. Handstand quarter turn dismount.
6. Handstand, squat, straddle or stoop dismount.
7. Double leg shoot through to stand on low bar.
8. Cast to straddle stand or free straddle support.

SINGLE LEG STEM RISE (Fig. 257)

PT Grasp high bar with a forward grip. Place right foot on the low bar and extend left leg upward so that ankle contacts the high bar. Keeping arms straight, extend right leg (forcing hips backward); then forcefully push down on the high bar while moving right leg vertically to bring hips to bar. Right foot

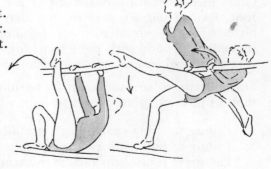

Figure 257

remains on low bar until body is almost to the front support position. Rotate grip, fully extend arms and shoulders, lift head and chest, and finish in a front support position.

SP Stand under high bar on performer's left side. Place inside hand on hips and outside hand on right leg to assist in backward and upward movement.

CE 1. Failure to extend right leg (causing backward movement of the hips) as body is being pulled to the high bar by arms.
  2. Not allowing arms to bend very slightly to get shoulders over bar before getting into the front support position.
  3. Allowing right foot to stop pushing on or to leave the low bar before the body is ready to go into the front support position.
  4. Failure to rotate grip, to extend arms and shoulders fully, and to end in a front support position.

MO Same as for double stem rise.

KIP FROM LOW TO HIGH BAR (Fig. 258)

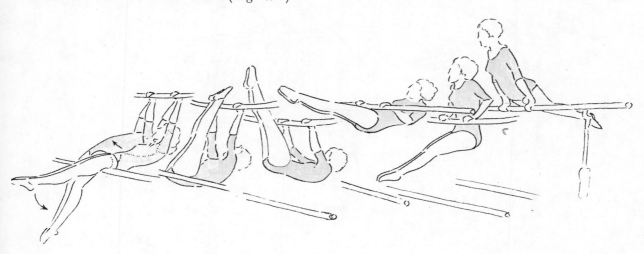

Figure 258

PT From rear support on low bar, grasp high bar with a forward grip. Keep eyes focused on high bar or on object in back of high bar until kipping action is almost completed; then look over high bar. Bring ankles to high bar; then forcefully move legs upward and simultaneously push down on the high bar with hands to bring hips to the high bar. As legs are moving up the bar, then outward, hips are extending. Rotate grip forward, extend arms and shoulders, and end in front support.

SP Place inside hand on back of upper thigh, outside hand on shoulder or upper back, and assist in entire movement to the front support.

CE 1. Allowing head to be forward.
  2. Sluggish movement throughout the skill.
  3. Kipping downward rather than upward, then outward (failure to force legs up the bar).
  4. Allowing arms to bend (except during rotation of hands to move to front support position).
  5. Failure to rotate grip, extend arms and shoulders, and end in a front support.

MO Same as from stem rise.

PT   From front support on high bar with hands in a forward grip, allow the upper body to drop backward (arms remaining straight), keeping thighs as close to the bar as possible. As the body moves under the bar, slightly bend the arms, lift left leg and lower right leg so that it is extended behind the low bar and left leg is extended in front of the low bar. Extend hips forward, bend arms, and lower body to stride position on low bar with control.

Figure 259

SP   Stand under high bar and support hips with outside hand and back of upper thigh of left leg with inside hand.

CE 1. Failure to keep arms straight as body drops behind the high bar.
      2. Failure to keep thighs close to the bar on the underswing.
      3. Failure to bend arms and control underswing as body passes under the high bar.
      4. Failure to extend hips as forward leg passes over the low bar.
      5. Failure to lower body to stride support with control.

MO 1. Maintain grip on high bar.
        a. Pullover low to high.
        b. Single or double stem rise after bringing back leg to the bar.
        c. Bring back leg over bar to rear sitting (hanging) support and kip to high bar.
      2. Change hands to low bar.
        a. Mill circle.
        b. Mill circle catch.
        c. Single leg flank dismount with quarter turn.

FORWARD ROLL TO REAR SEAT SUPPORT ON LOW BAR (Fig. 260)

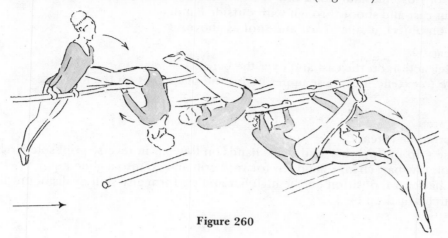

Figure 260

PT From front support on the high bar with hands in a forward grip, lower body forward (pike), rotate grip forward, and slowly lower body to rest on back of upper thighs on the low bar. Hands remain in a forward grip throughout the entire skill.

SP Stand between bars. Put outside hand on back as pike is achieved and inside hand on back of upper thigh to help lower to low bar.

CE 1. Bending legs.
      2. Failure to rotate grip.
      3. Failure to maintain a forward grip throughout entire skill.
      4. Failure to control movement to rear sitting support on low bar.

MO 1. Maintain grip on high bar.
        a. Pullover low to high bar.
        b. Single or double stem rise.
        c. Kip from low to high bar.
      2. Change grip to low bar.
        a. Front or back seat circle.
        b. Drop back and up.
        c. Dislocate into glide kip—catch high bar.

DOUBLE LEG SHOOT THROUGH TO STAND ON LOW BAR (Fig. 261)

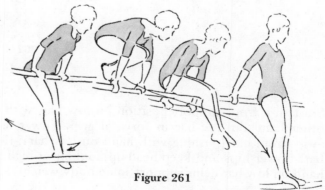

Figure 261

PT From a front support on the high bar with hands in a forward grip, cast away from the bar, keeping head up and shoulders forward of the bar. Immediately tuck knees to chest and extend legs over the high bar; extend hips and place toes on low bar; then extend upper body.

Hint: Place mat over the low bar to prevent bruises on legs if feet should miss the low bar. Also student should be able to control the squat stand and double leg shoot through to L support on low bar before attempting this skill on the high bar.

SP 1. Stand on low bar and hook one leg over the top bar. Support arm with inside hand and assist in cast and shoot through with outside hand.
2. Stand on object at side of bar and spot as above.

CE 1. Poor cast.
2. Slow leg action on the cast and over the bar.
3. Failure to extend hips, raise upper body, and place toes on the low bar.
4. Panic.

MO 1. Dislocate.
2. Back straddle catch.
3. Release grip on high bar and place hands on low bar in reverse grip; sole circle (stoop position) on low bar; change hands to forward grip and go into a glide kip.
4. Jump back to L position on the high bar and perform any skill or dismount listed from the seat circles or drop backs.

SQUAT STAND ON LOW BAR—(One hand on each bar—front support on low bar facing high bar) (Fig. 262)

Figure 262

PT Start in a front support position on low bar, with one hand on high bar in forward grip and other hand on low bar in forward grip. Lower legs down and forward; then forcefully cast away from bar (pushing with hand on low bar); flex hips, bend knees, and place toes on low bar. Lower hips and keep head up, looking at high bar. Hand on high bar assists in pulling, and hand on low bar helps support some body weight.

SP Start to either side of the low bar. Place hands in the hip area as cast is made. Help by lifting hips up so performer can *place* toes on bar.

CE 1. Insufficient cast and lift of hips (will hit shins on bar if cast too low).
2. Not using arms in push and pull action.

MO 1. Jump into straddle sole circle underswing half turn.
2. Stoop hop half turn to high bar.
3. Half turn back straddle catch.

RELEASES

CAST FROM HIGH BAR TO HIP CIRCLE ON LOW BAR (cast wrap) (Fig. 263)

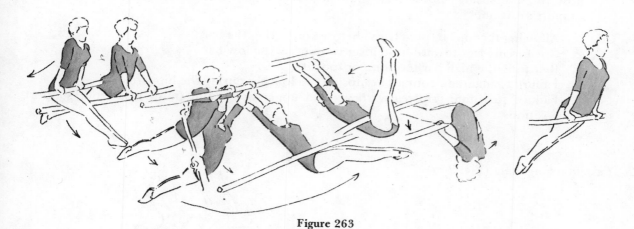

Figure 263

Lead-up:

First learn hip circle from the long hang, then the cast to the long hang to the hip circle on the low bar.

1. *Hip circle from long hang* (Fig. 264)

Figure 264

PT   Hang on high bar. Spotter between bars will initiate swing. As the performer contacts the low bar in a long hang position, she will forcefully pike (bringing knees toward head). When and only when this tight pike position is attained should the performer release the high bar to regrasp the low bar and continue with the hip circle. It might be advisable to have a certain number of swings and pikes before releasing the high bar, such as release on third contact with low bar. As movement continues around the low bar, there is a slight bend of the arms to allow the performer to constantly pull hips to the low bar (as in the hip circle from the cast). As the movement is almost completed, rotate the grip, extend arms and shoulders, head up, and finish in a front support.

SP One spotter between bars initiates swing by pushing hips toward the low bar. As the piked position is achieved, the other spotter in front of low bar places hands on backs of upper thighs to force body around the bar. As performer is reaching the front support position, the inside spotter can grasp legs and upper arm to help her maintain front support position.

CE 1. Allowing the hips to pike (flex) before contacting the bar.
      2. Not forcing legs toward head after contacting the low bar.
      3. Releasing the high bar too soon or too late.
      4. Failure to maintain contact of hips on the low bar during the hip circle.
      5. Failure to rotate grip rearward, extend upper body, and finish in a front support position.

2. *Cast to a long hang* (Fig. 265)

Figure 265

PT From a front support position on the high bar with the hands in a forward grip, bring legs forward under the bar; force legs backupward and extend arms to push body away from the bar with control. Keep body in a fully extended position and swing under the high bar toward the low bar.

Note: Leg action does not have to be very forceful if arms are extended properly. The important thing to remember is to extend arms so the entire body weight will not have to be supported by hands and shoulders in a jarring or jerky movement to the long hang position.

SP Stand behind the high bar and grasp legs and lower body throughout the swing. A second spotter can stand under the high bar to assist the performer if she loses her grip and to stop momentum of the swing by placing her hands on performer's abdomen.

CE 1. Jerky cast—allowing arms to bend, knees to bend, or legs to separate.
      2. Failure to keep body tight throughout long hang.

At this point, if student feels confident that she can perform each part of the skill by herself, the two may be combined. One spotter should spot the cast to the long hang, and the other one should spot the hip circle.

    CE of combined skills:
        1. Jerky or insufficient cast.
        2. Failure to keep body tight until hips have contacted the low bar.
        3. Failure to flex hips when they contact the low bar.
        4. Releasing the high bar too soon or too late.
        5. Failure to rotate grip, extend arms, raise upper body, and end in a front support.

    MO 1. Skills listed from front support position.
        2. Eagle catch.
        3. "Pop" glide kip.
        4. Hecht dismount.

DISLOCATE

This skill can be performed from two positions: stand on low bar and jump into pike position under high bar or from L position on low or high bar going into a partial forward seat circle.

Lead-up:

Stand on mat in front of low bar with back to bar. Lift arms sideways and grasp the low bar in an eagle grip. Bend knees and jump into a pike position under the bar (as if to perform forward roll). At this point the spotter can stand between the bars and move the student through the dislocate by slowly pulling her legs backward (at this point student lifts head up) and then lowering them to the mat as shoulders dislocate. Look at knees while in the pike position; as soon as hip is extended (legs going back), lift head.

From stand on low bar (Fig. 266)

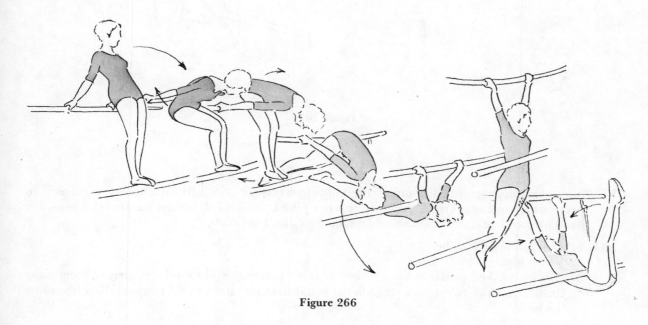

Figure 266

PT Stand on low bar and reach back to grasp the high bar with the eagle grip. Bend knees and jump up and forward into a pike position (roll hips overhead). Body now in pike under high bar. Eyes looking at knees. Pause very slightly to make sure the pike is attained; then lift head up and back and extend body fully into the long hang, allowing shoulders to dislocate. Continue with a hip circle on the low bar.

SP Stand under the high bar. As the performer jumps into the pike position, reach toward the back area to prevent a fall. As the body extends, place inside hand on upper thighs, and outside hand will support the back area just before performer goes into hip circle.

CE 1. Failure to jump up and forward when going into the pike position (so that hips will not hit the high bar and an effective swing can be developed).
2. Failure to eye spot knees when piked, then force head up and back as body extends and shoulders dislocate.
3. Failure to keep body in tight pike prior to body extension and dislocation of shoulders.
4. Failure to maintain straight arms throughout skill.
5. Extension of body and dislocation too early or too late.

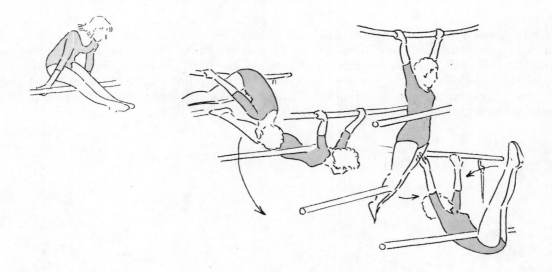

Figure 267

PT Support body weight on hands with hands in a reverse grip. Lift hips back-upward as if to perform a front seat circle. As body reaches piked position under the bar, extend hips, lift head up and back, dislocate shoulders, and go into long hang.

MO 1. Hip circle on low bar.
2. Drop kip.
3. Go into piked position on low bar as if to perform a hip circle, return to long hang position, beat swing and straddle or squat over low bar to rear support. Kip from low to high.

BACK STRADDLE CATCH (Fig. 268)

Lead-up:

Remove one bar from a set of even parallel bars and lower the remaining bar. Stand on a stack of mats or some other stable object that will make the distance from the mat to the bar equal to that of the low to the high bar and *touch* bar with one hand palm down for balance. Bend knees and spring *vertically* and backward, moving legs to a wide straddle position. Immediately grasp the bar between legs with both hands in a forward grip. The first few times the spotter should stop the performer in a straddle position on the bar. This will assure both spotter and performer that the jump, straddle, and grasp of the bar are being executed correctly. Also gives the performer confidence. When performer feels confident enough, the spotter can assist her to clear the bar and come to a stand on the mats behind the bar with hands still in contact with the bar.

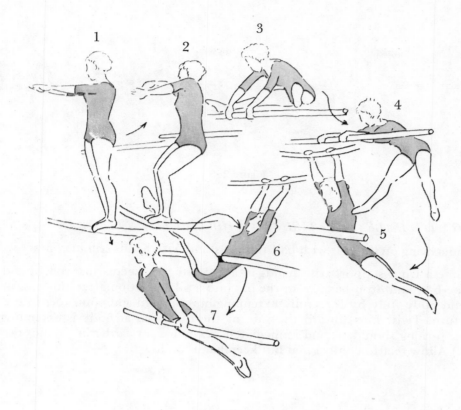

Figure 268

SP Spotter reaches over bar and grasps waist of performer. When she is ready to clear the bar, assist her by lifting and pulling hips back.

PT The performer should now transfer this skill to a regulation set of unevens. (If necessary, the spotter can stand on a long horse or some other stable object behind the high bar.) Jump vertically lifting hips up and back. Lift legs to a wide straddle position. Immediately grasp the high bar after the jump and straddle. Force heels out and back as legs come together to enable body to reach a fully extended position before going into the long hang position.

SP Stand in back of high bar and as performer straddles and grasps the bar, reach for or make contact with back of upper thighs to prevent a fall or to slow the long hang swing action until the student is able to perform the skill without contact spotting.

CE 1. Jumping back rather than vertical then back (letting hips drift back toward the bar before jumping), failure to keep upper body over feet.
2. Not grasping the bar with both hands simultaneously and immediately after jumping and straddling.
3. Insufficient straddle and failure to lift feet high enough to insure clearing the bar.
4. Failure to force heels back after clearing the bar to come into the long hang with a fully extended body.

MO Hip circle on the low bar and then any skill from that position, such as an eagle catch, drop kip, hecht, free front hip circle.

VA *Half turn back straddle to kip on same bar* (Fig. 269).

Figure 269

UNDERSWING WITH HALF (180°) TURN TO A HIP CIRCLE ON LOW BAR

Lead-up 1. Underswing on low bar with half turn to stand with hands still in contact with bar.

PT Assume a front support with hands in a forward grip; keep arms straight and thighs close to the bar, and drop back from the bar into a pike position after hips pass under the bar; extend body fully by forcefully extending hips upward and point toes in the direction of the turn. Twist hips toward the side of the turn, and as body is extending release one hand, turning shoulders, and immediately grasp in a forward grip. (Hands now in a mixed grip.) Allow feet to contact mat but keep hands on low bar.

Lead-up 2. *Sit on low bar facing high bar, hands on the high bar in a forward grip or mixed grip* (Fig. 270).

Figure 270

PT Lift ankles toward the high bar and immediately extend hips (entire body) and slightly bend arms to assist in upward and then outward extension of the body. Just as body reaches full extension, initiate the turn with hips and shoulders, leading the turn with toes. Release one hand (if turning toward left side, release right hand) and regrasp high bar in a forward grip. (Hands are now in a mixed grip.) Continue into long hang toward the low bar. May also start with mixed grip as shown in Fig. 270.

SP (Performer turning left) Stand between bars to right side of performer. Assist the half turn by placing hands on hips and turning hips to the left. Performer will release right hand. As the turn is completed, a second spotter can step in and assist performer through the long hang by placing hand on abdomen and upper thigh.

UNDERSWING WITH HALF TURN FROM FRONT SUPPORT ON HIGH BAR (back facing low bar) (Fig. 271)

Figure 271

PT Drop back from bar keeping thighs close to bar and arms straight. Pike, then extend body fully, make half (180°) turn, and go into long hang.

CE 1. Failure to keep thighs close to bar as underswing is initiated.
2. Failure to maintain straight arms throughout skill.
3. Failure to fully extend hips to force body upward and outward before the turn.
4. Turning too soon or too late.
5. Failure to maintain full body extension with feet well behind body when coming into the long hang toward the low bar.

MO 1. Hip circle on the low bar.
2. Any other skill listed from the long hang position.

VA 1. *Sole circle* (Fig. 272)

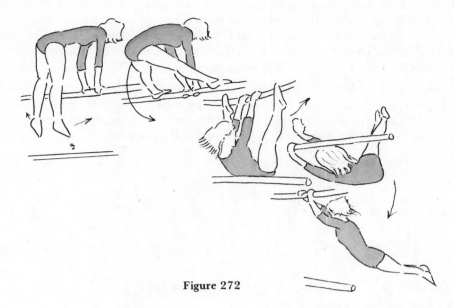

Figure 272

PT From a stand on the low bar facing the high bar with the hands in a forward grip, jump into a straddle stand position on the high bar (insteps on bar); pause momentarily, then underswing half turn into long hang, then hip circle on low bar.

Hint: It is very important in this skill to keep shoulders and arms fully extended and pull against the bar with the arms on the underswing to keep feet on the bar; also feet (ankles) must extend and push against the bar. Keep feet on the bar until the last possible moment, then extend legs with a foreupward thrust of hips to fully extend body before the turn.

2. *Underswing with half turn from free straddle support* (Fig. 273)

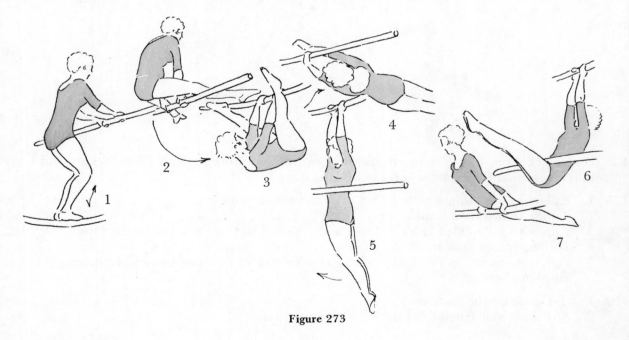

Figure 273

PT Stand on the low bar facing the high bar, hands in a forward grip; jump into a free straddle support position (legs over the bar), underswing, half turn into long hang.

UNDERSWING HALF TURN TO HIP CIRCLE ON LOW BAR FACING IN (Fig. 274)

Figure 274

PT Same principles as all other underswings—only difference is direction.

CE 1. Not riding hips up high enough over low bar.
2. Piking before hitting the low bar. (Should keep hips forward until contact; then pike into hip circle.)

SP Between bars—assist in slowing movement before hips hit bars by placing hands on abdomen and upper thigh.

EAGLE CATCH (Fig. 275)

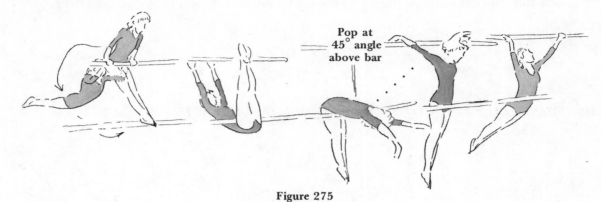

Figure 275

Lead-up:
   From a relaxed hang at hips over the low bar, spotter rocks performer forward and backward. On a prearranged signal, e.g., three swings, the performer forcefully lifts the upper body and swings arms vigorously forward sideways and backward to grasp the high bar in an eagle grip. As the upper body lifts, feet are forced backward so that the performer can pop off the low bar in an arched position. *Performer must not look for the high bar* but should tilt head upward on the pop and look directly forward.

SP   Stand between bars and grasp performer around upper thighs and help lift to high bar.

PT   From a very tight wrap in a hip circle on the low bar, as the body completes approximately three quarters of the hip circle, forcefully lift upper body, force heels backward, tighten hips and reach up, out and back to grasp the high bar in an eagle grip. As body reaches 45° angle from bar, pop begins.

SP   As performer is coming off the low bar, place inside hand on front of upper thigh and outside hand on hips or lower back.

CE   1. Popping too soon or too late.
   2. Insufficient pop—not forceful enough.
   3. Turning head to look at high bar.
   4. Failure to keep reaching back until hands contact bar.

EAGLE CATCH—DROP KIP (Fig. 276)

Figure 276

PT   From the eagle catch, the arms pull so shoulders can be lifted; the hips drive backward; then the hands release high bar to catch low bar. Legs can straddle or remain straight for the glide kip.

SP Stand between bars. As catch is made place inside hand on upper thigh and outside hand on back and assist by slightly supporting body weight until hands catch low bar.

CE 1. Not forcing heels back and keeping body tight in general on eagle.
2. Holding onto high bar too long.
3. Failure to push hips backward when dropping for kip.

DROP BACK FLANK CUT CATCH ON HIGH BAR (Fig. 277)

Lead-up: Flank cut dismount—described under dismounts.

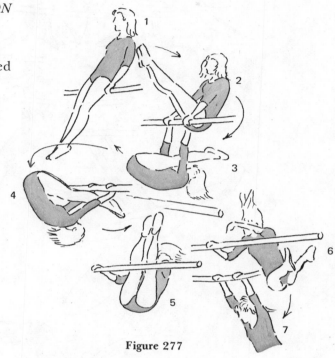

Figure 277

PT From L support position on the high bar with the hands in a forward grip, lift knees toward head (without bending legs) so that body is in a tight pike. Drop back under the bar in this position, maintaining straight arms. As body swings under the bar, maintain a tight pike position, pump hips back and, as the body begins upward movement (toward original position), push on the bar forcefully to raise body almost to the original position before flanking legs to the left. Keeping the upper body erect, force both legs to the left side after releasing left hand. Extend hips fully, regrasp the high bar, and continue into the long hang. After legs have flanked to the left, focus eyes over the high bar and keep focused there until hand regrasps the bar and the long hang is under way.

SP As the performer goes into an underswing pike position, the spotter may grasp hips or backs of upper thighs and assist the upward pumping movement before flanking. If the flank is to be executed to he left side, then spotter must stand to the right of the performer.

CE 1. Failure to keep arms straight throughout the skill.
2. Failure to keep body (except hands) free of the bar throughout the skill.
3. Failure to force knees to head and remain in a deep pike until flank is executed.
4. Failure to push against bar with hands to get as high as possible before flanking.
5. Failure to keep upper body erect during flank cut.
6. Failure to extend hips as legs clear the bar so that the body will be in a fully extended position before going into long hang.

MO Any skill from a long hang position mentioned previously.

VA *Drop back straddle cut catch* (Fig. 278)

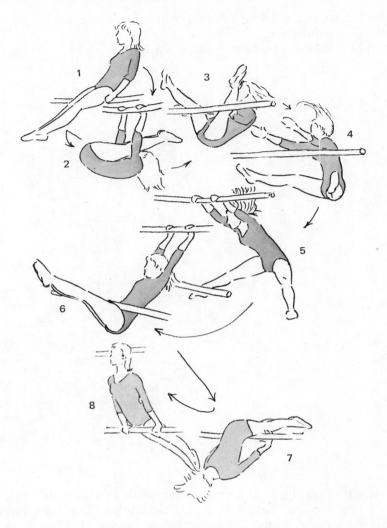

Figure 278

Lead-up: Drop back straddle cut dismount—described in dismounts.

PT   Technique is the same as for the flank cut catch except that the legs straddle and both hands leave the bar and regrasp; eyes look directly at the bar when straddling.

SP   Spotter stands directly behind the performer. Place hands on back of upper thighs to assist in straddle.

STOOP CATCH FORWARD (Fig. 279).

PT   Start with soles of feet on bars and hands in reverse grip. Push against bar with feet and pull with hands as body moves forward. Eyes can look at knees until hips pass under bar; then look for high bar. Stay in tight pike position until three-quarters circle completed; then release hands from low bar to catch high bar.

Figure 279

SP Stand in front of low bar and, as performer moves forward, place inside hand on back and outside hand on upper thigh. As body continues under bar, duck under bar (with hands still in same place) and assist with a lifting action until performer catches high bar.

CE 1. Starting with tip of toes on bar. (When going forward in a sole circle, you should start with the middle of the foot on the bar and, when going backward, start with the toes on the bar.)
2. Failure to extend legs and arms (especially in shoulder area) throughout entire skill.

MO 1. Double stem rise.
2. Drop kip.

VA 1. Straddle sole circle catch.
2. Straddle sole circle half turn catch.

STOOP HALF TURN CATCH (stoop hop half turn) (Fig. 280)

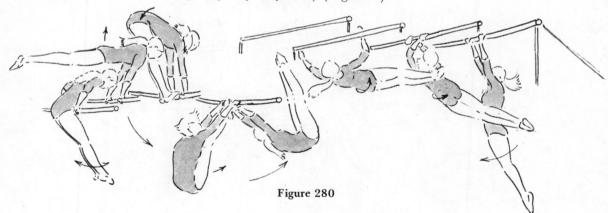

Figure 280

PT From front support on low bar cast to stoop position on low bar (on toes). Shift hands (in forward grip) slightly forward before backward motion begins. Keeping legs and arms completely straight, drop back in tight pike position. Look at knees at this point. As body passes under the bar, feet leave bar and shoot upward and outward. At this point hips are extended forcefully and eyes look for high bar. Both hands release low bar with right hand swinging across body to back of high bar, catching in forward grip, and left hand catches high bar in reverse grip as body completes half turn. Keep legs together and tight through skill.

SP Stand in front of low bar. As performer drops back in stoop position, place inside hand on upper thigh and outside hand on lower back. As body goes under bar, duck under keeping hands in contact with performer and assist with the lift and turn by pushing hip and back area.

CE 1. Bending arms or legs on stoop under bar.
2. Failure to extend hips and shoot legs up and out after passing under bar.
3. Holding onto low bar too long and failure to look for the high bar.

Hint: Learn stoop catch first before adding half turn.

MO 1. Hip circle on low bar.
2. Straddle or stoop legs over low bar; then kip to high bar.
3. Lift toes to low bar, change grip, stem to high bar.
4. Drop kip.

PARTIAL BACK SEAT CIRCLE TO DROP KIP ON LOW BAR (from L support facing low bar) (Fig. 281)

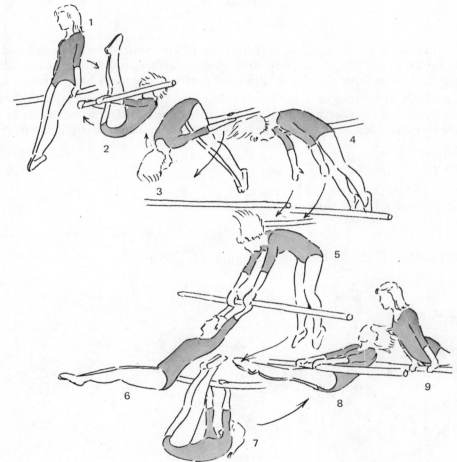

Figure 281

PT From an L support on the high bar, hands in a forward grip, drop back and perform a partial seat circle. Look at knees. Before forward movement begins (in the piked position), tilt head up and back so eyes can spot the low bar. Release the high bar, partially extend hips so that body is at a 90° angle, and drop to the low bar grasping bar with a forward grip. Go into a glide position and kip to the low bar.

SP Stand between the bars. As the performer is reaching the piked position under the bar and is ready to slightly extend and drop to the low bar, place inside hand on back and have outside hand ready to place on back of upper thigh. Use two spotters.

CE 1. Tensing up on back seat circle portion of skill.
2. Failure to look up and back after reaching piked position under bar and looking for low bar.
3. Failure to keep hips flexed (at 90°) when dropping to catch the low bar.
4. Not completing enough of the back seat circle, or completing too much of the back seat circle (riding it up too far).
5. Failure to release high bar and regrasp low bar in forward grip.

VA From rear support on low bar, hands in forward grip on high bar, kip to high bar with double leg shoot through, drop back under, and drop to kip on low bar.

PARTIAL BACK SEAT CIRCLE, EXTEND OVER LOW BAR TO DROP KIP ON LOW BAR, END FACING HIGH BAR (Fig. 282)

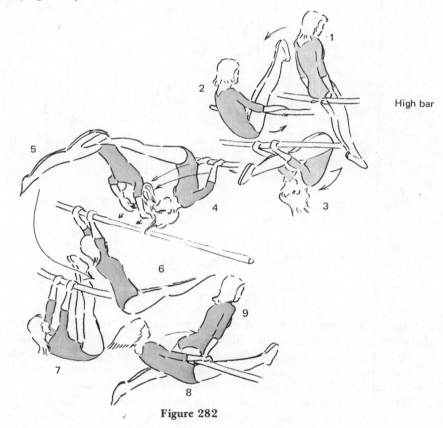

Figure 282

PT From L support on high bar with back to low bar, hands in a forward grip, drop back as if to perform a partial back seat circle, eyes looking at knees. As forward movement begins from the piked position under the bar, partially extend hips so body is at a 90° angle. Pass over the low bar in this position, tilting head to look at the low bar. Release high bar and grasp low bar in a forward grip. Keep arms extended and glide under low bar; then kip to low bar.

SP Two spotters, one between bars, one outside low bar. Spotter between the bars should grasp shoulder with inside hand and front of upper thigh with outside hand and help performer over the low bar. Spotter on outside of bar should place outside hand on lower back and inside hand on back of upper thigh and help to glide kip. Should use four spotters to begin with.

Lead-up: From L support on low bar, drop back and practice extending in 90° angle to stand on mat.

CE 1. Failure to begin forward movement from piked position before slightly extending hips and looking for low bar.
  2. Extending hips too much on shoot over low bar (opening body too much).
  3. Failure to release high bar as body extends (slightly) to pass over low bar.
  4. Failure to grasp low bar in a forward grip, maintain open pike, and continue into glide kip.

HANDSTAND PIROUETTE (handstand half turn) (Fig. 283)

Figure 283

PT Can be done with hands in forward grip or mixed grip. Stand on low bar with hands on high bar in forward grip. Press hips into high bar then away. Bend knees, flex hips, and forcefully push off of low bar with legs and feet. Keeping arms straight, force hips upward with legs in a straddle position. As hips reach overhead position bring legs together to fully stretched handstand position. As body passes vertical point, start rotation with right shoulder, release the left hand, and regrasp bar; then change right hand to forward grip. Keep body tight throughout. (Do not allow body to have large arch in back.) When pressing into handstand keep head up and back. When starting the half turn, look at the bar or hands.

SP 1. In beginning: Stand on low bar with one foot, other leg hooked over high bar. Hold upper arm with your inside hand and lift in hip area with outside hand. Have someone on mat to slow down momentum or swing into the low bar.
  2. After confidence is built up: Stand to back of high bar to assist in control of swing coming into low bar.

Hint: To learn handstand, pile mats in front of low bar to assimilate distance and height to high bar. Jump from mats into handstand on low bar. Could also use parallel bars. Take off one bar, lower other and use mats stacked up. Also it is to performer's advantage to learn the handstand quarter turn dismount off high bar before adding half turn.

CE 1. Insufficient push with legs to get to handstand position.
2. Failure to keep arms straight.
3. Trying to bring legs together from straddle position before hips are over hands.
4. Not keeping body tight after handstand position is reached.

MO 1. Hip circle on low bar; then anything from that position.
2. Hecht dismount.
3. Hit low bar, back uprise or drop kip.

DISMOUNTS

SINGLE LEG FLANK WITH QUARTER (90°) TURN (Fig. 284)

Figure 284

PT Assume a stride position on the low bar, right leg in front, right hand in a reversed grip, left hand in either a forward or reversed grip. Lift (flank) left leg sideways, upward, and over the bar. As leg is being lifted, support weight with right hand, and take left hand off the bar and lift it sideways. As left leg passes over the bar, extend hips, execute quarter turn and land on mat with right hand still contacting bar. Turn head to right and land with knees slightly bent to absorb shock and for balance.

SP Stand behind performer on supporting arm side. Place outside hand on elbow of left arm and have inside hand ready to help lift right leg and clear bar.

CE 1. Failure to lift leg high enough to clear bar and to keep legs straight at all times.
2. Failure to keep supporting arm (right in this case) straight at all times.
3. Failure to lift arm as leg passes over bar.
4. Failure to extend hips as leg passes over bar.
5. Failure to keep upper body erect at all times.
6. Failure to maintain contact with the bar with supporting hand until feet have reached the mat and balance is attained.

VA Single leg flank dismount with three-quarter turn.

UNDERSWING ON LOW BAR (Fig. 285)

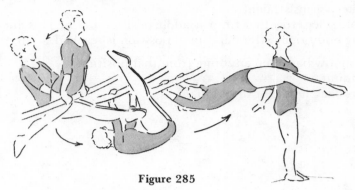

Figure 285

PT From a front support position on the low bar with a forward grip, keep arms straight, thighs close to the bar, and drop back behind the bar, lifting legs upward. After hips pass under the bar, fully extend body by thrusting hips and legs foreupward, then outward as hands release the bar. Land with knees slightly bent, arms over head, and head between arms.

SP Stand in front of low bar beside performer. Reach under bar with inside hand and grasp performer's back. As the underswing begins, place outside hand on back of the upper thighs to help lift legs upward. Maintain contact until the performer has landed.

CE 1. Failure to keep arms straight as body drops back, then to bend arms slightly as body is extending to push body away from bar.
2. Failure to lift legs upward to keep thighs close to the bar until hips pass under the bar.
3. Failure to push away from the bar (release the hands) as body extends upward and outward.
4. Allowing upper body to fall forward upon landing (mainly due to allowing hips to flex).

VA 1. *Underswing from high bar over low bar* (Fig. 286)

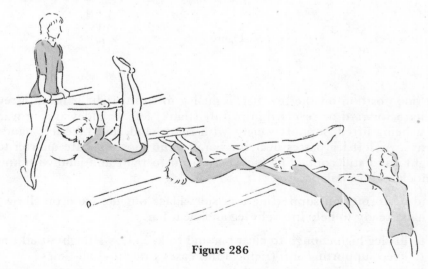

Figure 286

PT Same principles of movement as for underswing from low bar.

SP One spotter between bars to help clear low bar; place inside hand on hip, outside hand on upper back. Second spotter, in front of bar, places inside hand on hip as performer is clearing the bar and outside hand on back of upper thigh. Maintain contact until landing position is achieved.

2. *Underswing from high bar over low bar with half (180°) turn* (Fig. 287)

Figure 287

PT Underswing from front support on high bar; as body reaches fully extended position, make half turn leading with toes and turning hips in the direction of the turn. If the turn is being made to the left, head should turn to the left as the turn is initiated. Performer should land facing low bar.

SP Same as for preceding underswing variation. Spotter in front of bar stands at nonturning side of performer.

3. Underswing may also be performed with quarter or three-quarter turn.

HANDSTAND QUARTER (90°) TURN FROM FRONT SUPPORT ON HIGH BAR (Fig. 288)

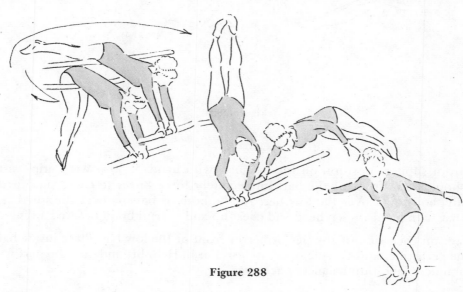

Figure 288

PT From a front support position on the high bar, flex upper body and grasp the low bar with left hand in a forward grip and right hand in a reverse grip (hands shoulder width apart). Lower legs and immediately swing them upward to move body into a handstand position on the low bar. As body slightly overbalances, initiate quarter (90°) turn by shifting weight to right straight arm and rolling hips to the right. Keep head up and back and, as turn is initiated, look to the right still keeping head up and back. Release left hand, lift upper body, and allow feet to land on mat. (There will be a slight hip flexion on descent.) Upon landing, right side of body will be facing the low bar, and right hand will remain on the low bar until balance is achieved.

SP One spotter stands between bars and helps the performer pass through a handstand position by pushing on abdomen. A second spotter stands between the bars to the right of the performer with both hands ready to make sure legs clear bar. A third spotter in front of low bar grasps performer's left arm to make sure hand does not leave the bar until she has landed properly.

CE 1. Failure to drop legs and forcefully swing them upward to allow body to reach handstand position before making the turn.
    2. Failure to keep arms straight at all times.
    3. Not releasing the left arm at all or too late.
    4. Failure to lift upper body and keep body fairly extended after the turn until landing.
    5. Failure to maintain contact with low bar until landing.

SQUAT VAULT OVER LOW BAR (Fig. 289)

Figure 289

PT From a front support position on the low bar, with hands in a forward grip, cast forcefully, keeping shoulders in front of the bar. Immediately force knees to chest, push with hands, lift upper body, and squat over the low bar. As the body is passing over the low bar, push away from the bar with hands. Keep head and chest up and extend body before landing.

SP One spotter on each side of the performer in front of the low bar. Place inside hand on upper arm of the performer and outside hand on lower arm. Help lift and pull the performer over the bar. Maintain contact until balance is achieved.

CE 1. Insufficient cast.
    2. Failure to lift head and chest and to push body away from the bar as legs pass over the bar.
    3. Failure to bring knees forcefully to chest on squat action.
    4. Failure to extend body before landing.

VA 1. Straddle vault over the low bar.
    2. Stoop vault over the low bar.

Note: The principles for the straddle and stoop are the same except for the action of the legs. Spotting is also the same as for the squat vault dismount.

HANDSTAND SQUAT, STOOP, OR STRADDLE (Fig. 290)

PT Squat. From front support on high bar, flex upper body and grasp low bar with hands in a forward grip, shoulder width apart. Lower legs and forcefully swing them upward so that the body leaves the high bar and moves into a handstand support position on the low bar. Overbalance slightly (heels past hands), keeping shoulders over hands, then squat, straddle or stoop, lifting the head and chest while forcefully pushing away from the low bar. Land in front of the low bar. Extend body fully before landing.

Figure 290

SP Same as for cast to squat vault over the low bar.

CE 1. Failure to maintain straight arms throughout skill.
2. Failure to keep head up when in handstand position.
3. Failure to forcefully thrust legs upward and over high bar to allow body to go through handstand position.
4. Failure to slightly overbalance before continuing with squat, straddle, or stoop.
5. Failure to lift head and chest and push body away from the bar as the squat, straddle, or stoop is executed over the low bar.
6. Failure to extend body before landing.
7. Failure to keep head up at all times.

DROP BACK FLANK CUT DISMOUNT (Fig. 291)

PT From L position on the high bar with the hands in a forward grip, lift knees toward head (as if to start a back seat circle) and, keeping arms straight, drop back and swing under the high bar in a pike position. As movement upward begins, push downward on the high bar to force body as far foreupward as possible. Keeping upper body erect, release left hand and allow legs to flank to the left side of body. When body is fully extended with feet under it, release right hand and land with knees slightly bent and slight hip flexion.

SP Same as for flank cut catch. Maintain contact until balance is achieved upon landing.

CE 1. Failure to keep arms straight throughout skill.
2. Failure to keep body (except hands) free of the bar throughout the skill.
3. Failure to stay in a pike position until the flank is executed.
4. Failure to push against the bar with hands to get as high as possible before flanking.
5. Failure to extend hips as body flanks and to push down on bar with right hand before releasing it to dismount.

Hint: Learn on low bar first.

VA *Drop back straddle cut dismount* (Fig. 292)

   PT From L support on high bar with hands in a forward grip, drop back and swing under high bar (same as in flank cut dismount). As back-

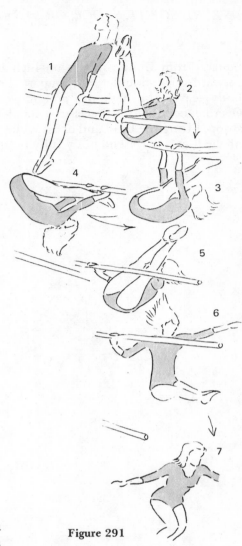

Figure 291

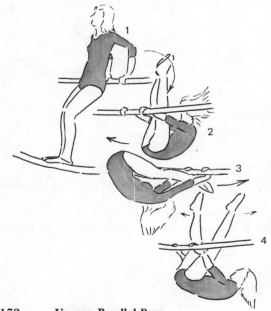

Figure 292

upward movement begins, forcefully push on high bar with hands to raise body as far as possible before legs straddle. It is very important to keep upper body erect when legs straddle and hands release bar.

SP   Same as for straddle cut catch. Maintain contact until balance is achieved upon landing.

HECHT (Fig. 293)

Figure 293

Lead-up:
   From a front support position on the low bar, relax in a piked hanging position. On a previously arranged signal between the performer and spotter, lift the upper and lower body *forcefully* and *simultaneously* while reaching foreupward with the arms. (This movement will be referred to as the pop.)

SP   One spotter on each side of the performer in front of the bar. Grasp the upper arm with outside hand before movement begins. As the popping action is made, pull the performer off the bar, placing inside hands on the performer's abdomen to help lift the entire body over the bar. Contact must be maintained until performer has landed properly.

Dismount:
PT   The hecht is usually prefaced with a cast (from a front support on the high bar) through the long hang position to a hip circle on the low bar, then off. After the skill has been mastered from the cast, then it may be performed from other skills, such as the back straddle catch-hecht dismount. It is essential to have a tight hip circle (so that the momentum developed in the cast to the long hang will not be lost) to allow the pop to be forceful enough to lift the body forward and up. As the body passes over the low bar, keep legs straight and hips tight. Keep lifting arms, head, and upper body so that legs and feet may be pulled under body to ensure proper landing. Popping action starts when upper body is at 45° angle to floor.

SP   After the hip circle is almost completed and the pop is about to occur, place inside hand on lower back and outside hand on abdomen and help lift and pull over the bar. Since this is a very fast move, the spotters must be very alert and ready to spot the performer if she should come off of the bar too soon or too late.

CE   1. Insufficient cast and poor hip circle.
      2. Popping too soon or too late.
      3. Failure to reach foreupward and to the side with arms and to continue reaching until feet are on the mat.
      4. Failure to keep body (especially hips) tight when popping.
      5. Lifting hips and allowing knees to bend when passing over the bar.
      6. Failure to keep head and upper body moving upward until feet have contacted mat.

VA *Straddle hecht*

    PT   Same technique as above; as popping action starts, straddle legs instead of keeping them together.

    SP   Use same spotting technique.

HECHT WITH FULL TWIST (Fig. 294)

Figure 294

PT   When the upper body reaches a 45° angle between the floor and low bar from the cast wrap, the popping action begins as if doing a regular hecht. At this point look to the left and force the right arm across the face. Keep the entire body taut with left arm close to chest, body will pass over bar. Notice that half of the turn is made as the body is popping upward and the remainder of the turn is made after clearing the bar. Just before landing, try to look at an object at eye level. Flex hips and knees slightly before landing.

SP   As popping action is about to occur, place inside hand on left waist and outside hand on right waist. Pull body with inside hand toward you and push with outside hand. As performer rotates hands will slide around waist area, regrasping opposite sides, then finishing with outside hand on abdomen and inside hand on lower back. The spotter must lift and quickly rotate the move forward so she does not stop the momentum of the performer.

CE   1. Turning too late or too soon.
        2. Not keeping body tight after "pop."
        3. Not using arms to assist in turn.

HANDSTAND QUARTER TURN DISMOUNT OFF HIGH BAR (Fig. 295)

PT   Stand on low bar, with hands in forward grip on high bar. Press hips into high bar, then away. At this point bend knees and flex hips and forcefully push off of low bar with legs and feet. Keeping arms straight, force hips upward with legs in a straddle position. As hips reach overhead position, bring legs together to fully stretched handstand position. As body passes vertical position, remove left hand and make quarter turn. As feet lower past high bar, keep eyes focused forward and release right hand. Land with hips and knees slightly flexed to absorb shock.

SP   In beginning stand on low bar with leg hooked over high bar. Hold upper arm with inside hand and lift in hip area with outside hand. Have someone on floor to back of performer to assist if she should fall backward on the landing. After skill is learned, stand behind bar and assist at waist area during landing.

Figure 295

CE 1. Insufficient push with legs to get to handstand position.
    2. Failure to keep arms straight and allowing back to arch.
    3. Not keeping entire body tight after hitting handstand position.

Routine Composition for Class

Since the majority of our girls are weak in the upper arm and shoulder area, routines for class should be composed of just a few skills at first. As strength and endurance are developed and skill ability is increased, the routines can be lengthened.

The routine should be composed of a mount, skills on one bar, skills going from one bar to the other (also facing each direction), and a dismount.

Some of the routines are partial routines and can be performed on one bar. This will give those students who do not have unevens a chance to perform a partial routine even though it involves skills on only one bar.

BEGINNING ROUTINES

1. Jump to front support, back hip circle, single leg flank to a stride support, single leg flank dismount with quarter turn.
2. Pullover on low bar, back hip circle, single leg flank to a stride support, mill circle, single leg flank dismount with quarter turn.
3. Stand facing low bar. Jump to front support, single leg flank to stride support, single leg swing down and up, grasp high bar, pullover on high bar, underswing to stride support on low, single leg flank dismount with quarter turn.
4. Stand facing low bar. Back pullover on low bar, back hip circle, single leg flank to stride support. Single stem to high bar, underswing to stride support on low bar, mill circle, single leg flank back to front support on low, underswing dismount.

5. Beat swing squat mount (to toes on bar), double leg stem rise to high bar, underswing to stride position on the low bar, mill circle, reach back grasp high bar, pull over to high bar. Forward roll to stride position on low bar, single stem rise to high bar, underswing dismount over low bar.

ADVANCED BEGINNING ROUTINES

1. Beat swing straddle mount, single stem to front support on high, cast to hip circle on low bar, single leg shoot through to stride position on low bar, mill circle catch high bar, back hip pullover to front support on high, back hip circle on high bar, handstand quarter turn dismount.
2. Stand outside bars facing high bar.
   Glide kip on low bar. Back hip circle, squat stand, stand and jump to front support on high bar, underswing on high with half turn to hip circle on low bar. Single leg shoot through to stride position, mill circle catch high bar. Single stem to high bar, handstand quarter turn dismount.
3. Stand outside bars.
   Glide kip to front support, squat stand, jump to free straddle support on high bar, underswing half turn to hip circle on low bar, single leg shoot through, mill circle catch, single stem to high bar, cast to hip circle on low bar, double leg shoot through, back seat circle, drop back and up to catch high bar, kip from low to high, double leg shoot through and flank dismount.

Routine Composition for Competition

Routines on the uneven parallel bars should consist of swinging movements from one bar to the other. Approximately ten to sixteen skills, including the mount and dismount, should be used in a sequence that will take the performer under and over both bars and in both directions. Skills that require the performer to release the bar and regrasp the same bar or the other bar are more desirable.

The performer should include six elements of difficulty, two of which must be of superior difficulty (refer to FIG Code of Points). All skills should flow from one to the other, with planned hesitations *only* before extremely difficult movements.

Performers should try to be creative when developing their routines since credit is given for originality.

INTERMEDIATE ROUTINES

1. Stand between bars facing low bars.
   Glide kip catch high bar, drop kip with double leg shoot through to rear support. Forward seat circle catch the high bar, kip from low to high, free back hip circle to long hang into hip circle on low bar, eagle catch. Squat onto low bar, back straddle catch, hecht dismount.

2. (Approach from behind high bar) Run and dive into front hip circle, cast to stoop position, sole circle forward catch high bar, drop kip to low, catch high bar. Beat swing stoop over low bar to rear support, kip to high bar. Double leg shoot through, dislocate, hip circle on low to eagle, drop kip and catch the high bar, stoop legs over the low bar to rear seat support, kip with double leg shoot through and immediately straddle cut dismount.

3. The routine done in Figure 296 is as follows:

1-4	Kip, double leg shoot through catch high bar
5-13	Kip, double leg shoot through to high bar with partial back seat circle drop to low bar kip, catch high bar
14-18	Double stem to high bar immediate stoop through
19-25	Drop back straddle cut catch to hip circle on low bar stopping momentarily in front support
26-37	Front hip circle, immediately stoop on low bar; change grip; stoop sole circle forward;

change grip kip with double leg shoot through over low bar catching high bar with right hand and low bar with left hand

38-40 Press to squat position and turn 180° to face high bar

41-45 Immediately jump to free aerial straddle and underswing with half turn to hip circle on low bar followed by eagle

46-51 Bring feet to low bar, push through to stand on low bar, then jump to underswing and straddle cut dismount

Figure 296

NOTES

CHAPTER SIX
SIDE HORSE VAULTING

Vaulting for girls can be a very exciting event because it involves the body floating momentarily through space before and after contacting the horse. Too often we find girls petrified of the horse; they frequently sound like broken records with, "It's too high," or "The board is too far back." These remarks are usually accompanied by jammed fingers, sore wrists, or ugly bruises on the shins. Incidents of this nature should not happen frequently if proper vaulting techniques and safety precautions are stressed from the beginning. There are, invariably, those girls who will not get over the horse before attempting the vaults fifty times; however, it should be remembered that all girls are not designed to be champion vaulters.

Special Conditioning Exercises

1. Consecutive vertical jumps from the balls of the feet.
2. Sprints.
3. Handstand snap downs (mule kicks) to a squat, stoop, and straddle stand.
4. Run and punch off board into layout dive roll on a crash pad.

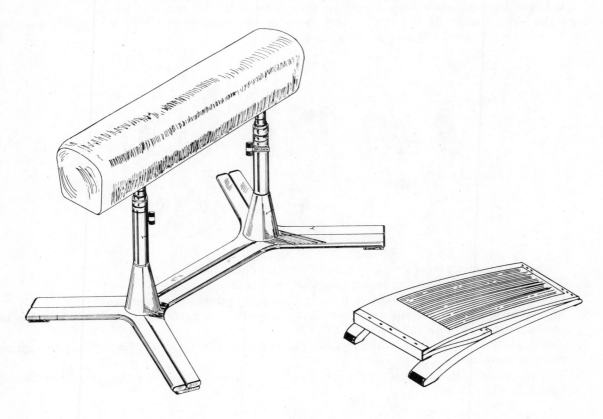

Safety Hints

1. Runway should be free of obstructions.
2. Frequently remove dust of any type or other slippery substances from the runway.
3. If necessary, rope off runway so that other people in the area will not interfere with the vaulters' run.
4. Proper shoes (gymnastic slippers with rubber soles) should be worn. Pads can be inserted in the shoes to minimize sore feet and shin splints.
5. Use damp towel or resin to step on before running to prevent slipping.
6. Reuther board should have rubber grips on the bottom to prevent it from sliding, or use a board spacer.
7. Use mats (double thickness when possible) or crash pad on far side of horse where vaulters normally land.
8. Two or more spotters should be used, especially for beginners.
9. Performers should inform spotters beforehand of the vault they intend to perform so that they may be in the correct position.
10. Use mats when possible on runway to help prevent shin splints.
11. Use trampoline to save wear and tear on legs when doing a lot of handspring vaults at one time.
12. Have a definite skill progression.

Vaulting Technique

Vaulting can be divided into four major categories:
1. Approach (run);
2. Takeoff (hurdle and contact with the reuther board);
3. On horse contact;
4. Afterflight and landing.

At the beginning level, our major concern should be with the run and takeoff. The run can determine the performance of the rest of the vault, so we must master this motor skill and be concerned with the following techniques for a good run.

RUN (Fig. 297)

Figure 297

PT 1. Slight forward lean with the head held in a natural position.
2. Eyes focused on the reuther board (place of foot contact).
3. Proper use of arms—foreupward and backupward in opposition to the legs.
4. Strong push downward and backward with balls of feet, never allowing heels to come in complete contact with the floor.
5. Adequate knee lift so that, when feet contact the floor, the push will be forceful enough to develop forward velocity.
6. Steady stride with increasing velocity, reaching maximum speed a few steps before the hurdle is taken.

CE 1. Body leans too far forward or backward.
    2. Run is flat footed.
    3. Arms not used properly.
    4. Knees turned in; heels out.
    5. Knees turned out.
    6. Run not forceful.
    7. Speed not increased gradually.

The distance or number of paces that each vaulter uses varies among individuals. To ensure a reasonable consistency in contacting the board, the distance should be carefully measured. This can be done by stepping off the number of feet or by using a tape measure. The distance should be long enough to allow the performer to reach maximum speed about fifteen feet (three to four steps) before the hurdle.

The speed of the run will vary with each performer, and to some degree it will depend on the vault to be executed.

After learning to run properly, add the hurdle and contact with the reuther board. It is advisable to learn the hurdle first from a step, then gradually add steps, from a slow run and finally from a vaulting run.

COMPONENTS OF A GOOD HURDLE AND TAKEOFF (Fig. 298 and 299)

Figure 298   Figure 299

PT 1. The hurdle should be long and not too high so as not to lose forward velocity and to maintain balance. As the hurdle step is taken, arms go down to sides of body.
    2. The knee lift is only slight to allow both legs to come together quickly.
    3. The balls of both feet must contact the board parallel and simultaneously with a very slight knee bend (heels never touch). Since the action of the reuther board is very fast, a great knee bend upon contact would cause a very long and (sluggish) takeoff.
    4. Shoulders should be slightly behind the toes when contact is made on the board.
    5. As feet contact the board, the arms reach forward and upward to assist on the vertical lift.
    6. Immediately extend knees explosively to ensure a high vertical lift.
    7. Ankle extension is also very important; extend ankles fully in order to allow the tips of the toes to leave the board last.
    8. As the hurdle step is taken, transfer eyes from the board to the horse or beyond the horse, depending upon the type of vault being executed.

CE 1. Hurdle too high, too low, too short, or a combination of any of these.
    2. Slowing the run before the hurdle.
    3. Bending the knees too much upon contacting the board.
    4. Landing flat footed on the board.
    5. Allowing the body to lean forward (mainly upper body) when feet contact the board.
    6. Little or no ankle or hip extension.
    7. Poor arm direction or uncoordinated arm and leg action.

Hint: Practice run and hurdle to a jump onto a stack of mats or the trampoline before using the horse.

The position of the body in preflight will be discussed under the individual vaults. It is essential that there be a visible distinction (time lapse) from reuther board contact to horse contact.

Usually *on horse contact* and *afterflight* are not mastered until the intermediate to advanced stage of vaulting; since all vaults involve these parts, however, it is essential to stress some of the basic components of the last half of the vault.

ON HORSE CONTACT

PT 1. On most vaults, the hands contact the horse shoulder distance apart and in the middle of the top of the horse.
2. When the hands contact the horse, the shoulders should be almost directly over the hands, sometimes behind, but *never forward of the hands*.
3. The touch on the horse should be of a very short duration.
4. The shoulders should never be allowed to sag as hands contact the horse.

CE 1. Hands on horse too long, usually resulting in downward slant after flight.
2. Insufficient push off the horse, or push poorly directed.
3. Other faults due to poor takeoff, such as contacting the horse on the near side (caused by a forward lean).

AFTERFLIGHT

In general, the greater the preflight and push, the greater the afterflight. The body should be extended in the air before landing; this mainly refers to squat, stoop, and straddle vaults. The afterflight should be upward as well as outward; a higher afterflight allows more time to position the body for a good landing.

LANDING

1. Landing should be solid but light.
2. Bend knees slightly to absorb shock and to help maintain balance.
3. Arms are slightly forward or sideward (obliquely) for balance, then to side when standing.
4. Slight forward bend of the body at hips.
5. If students can be taught to "stick" (stop upon making contact with mat) vaults, there will be fewer accidents.

Lead-up Skills

If a side horse is not available, other pieces of equipment can be used for teaching vaulting techniques.

1. Use a pile of mats (about two feet high) and have students take an abbreviated run and hurdle, landing on the mats.
2. Use mats as above and have students run, hurdle, and jump over the pile of mats.
3. Use lowered swedish box (2 to 2½ feet).
   a. Jump up to stand and off.
   b. Jump to squat stand and off.
   c. Squat vault.
   d. Jump to straddle stand, then off.
   e. Straddle vault.
4. Lower a balance beam and cover it with mats.
   a. Use same procedures as for swedish box.
   b. Use reuther board and raise beam slightly.

If a horse and reuther board are available from the beginning, be concerned with two things: how high should the horse be, and how far away from the horse should the board be (assuming that the girls have had ample practice on the run, hurdle and takeoff on the board to a mat)? Since quick success is a strong motivational factor in learning, lower the horse below standard height and place the board approximately two feet from the base of the horse.

Progression

JUMP TO SQUAT STAND ON HORSE (Fig. 300)

Figure 300

PT Take an abbreviated run and hurdle. After the vertical lift from the board, raise hips upward so that back is parallel to the floor and tuck knees to chest. Place the hands in the center (middle of top) of the horse with the hands shoulder width apart, arms straight, and fingers spread slightly. Lower hips and allow feet to come to rest on the horse between the hands. Lift chest as feet contact the horse, and focus eyes on object at eye level in front of the horse. Stand and jump off, bending knees when landing. Arms foreupward, then down.

SP Stand on far side of horse beside performer. Reach across the horse and grasp upper arm and wrist of the performer as she places hands on the horse. Be careful not to hinder her movement.

CE 1. Poor run and hurdle.
2. Landing on the board flat footed.
3. Leaning forward on the board.
4. Knees bending too much on the board, causing the forward momentum to be slowed down.
5. Insufficient vertical lift.
6. Poorly coordinated arms.
7. Placement of the hands on the near side of the horse rather than on the top.
8. Failure to lift hips and bring knees to chest. (Many beginners tend to bring the hips under the body rather than lifting them backupward.)
9. Failure to maintain straight arms and shoulders erect.

SQUAT VAULT FROM AN ABBREVIATED RUN (Fig. 301)

Figure 301

PT   After the vertical lift, *raise hips backupward* and tuck knees to chest. After reaching foreupward, place hands on top of the horse. Immediately push downupward on the horse, lifting chest; then lift arms foreupward. Eyes look at the board when running, horse when hurdling, and object at eye level in front of the horse when passing over the horse. As feet pass over the horse, extend legs and hips so that body is straight before landing. Land with hips and knees slightly flexed.

SP   Same as for squat stand. Maintain contact until the performer has gained balance upon landing.

CE   1.   Same as 1—9 for squat stand.
        2.   Allowing hands to remain on the horse as feet pass over the horse.
        3.   Failure to completely extend body before landing.
        4.   Failure to lift head and chest after pushing off the horse with hands.
        5.   Allowing arms to go over head and back upon landing (this causes many beginners to fall back toward the horse).

JUMP TO STRADDLE STAND (Fig. 302)

PT   From an abbreviated run, hurdle. On the vertical lift from the board, lift hips up and back; then force legs to a wide straddle position. As hands contact the horse, lift head and chest and allow feet to contact the horse in a wide straddle position. The shoulders will be slightly forward of the hands due to the stop on the horse in the straddle position.

Figure 302

SP   Stand on the far side of the horse in front of the performer. Reach across the horse and grasp upper arms as performer puts them on the horse. Assist by lifting and pulling to the horse, if necessary, and help control the straddle stand position.

CE   1.   Same as 1—7 of the squat stand.
        2.   Failure to lift hips high enough to allow feet to straddle onto the horse.
        3.   Failure to straddle both legs.
        4.   Failure to lift head and chest when feet come to rest on the horse.
        5.   Failure to maintain straight arms throughout the skill.

STRADDLE VAULT (Fig. 303)

Figure 303

PT From an abbreviated run, hurdle to the board and immediately spring vertically, lifting hips backupward. Reach foreupward with arms to place hands on the top of the horse (eyes look up at this point) while simultaneously straddling legs. Immediately push off the horse with hands and lift upper body. As legs pass over the horse, extend hips forward and bring legs together before landing. Land with knees and hips slightly flexed.

SP Stand in front of horse and performer (one foot slightly in front of the other). As the performer places hands on the horse, grasp her upper arms. As she is moving over the horse, step back and help lift and pull her to make sure she clears the horse. Maintain contact until proper landing.

CE 1. Same as 1—9 of straddle stand.
      2. Failure to maintain straight arms throughout skill.
      3. Failure to push off of the horse and keep shoulders erect almost immediately after contact.
      4. Failure to lift head and chest, extend hips, and bring legs together before landing.

BENT HIP ASCENT STOOP (Fig. 304)

Figure 304

PT After vertical lift from the board, raise hips as high as possible and focus eyes beyond the horse. Hands reach foreupward and then are placed on the top of the horse (wide enough apart to allow hips to pass through). Force straight legs through arms with an immediate push from the horse and forcefully lift head and chest. Extend hips forward to allow body to extend completely before landing.

SP Same as for squat vault.

CE 1. Poor run and hurdle.
2. Insufficient lift from board.
3. Failure to lift hips high on vertical lift from board.
4. Failure to maintain straight arms and legs throughout skill.
5. Failure to focus eyes beyond the horse upon hand contact on horse.
6. Failure to forcefully drive legs through arms, to push off the horse with hands, and to lift head and chest.
7. Failure to force hips forward to allow body to extend before landing.

Layout Vaulting

Once girls have mastered the layout position in vaulting, they have moved into the intermediate vaulting category. The following techniques are suggested as aids for developing a good layout position between the reuther board and the horse.

GENERAL TECHNIQUES

1. Develop a consistent run and take-off spot on the board.
2. Increase the speed of the run so that maximum speed will be reached just before the hurdle.
3. Move the board back from the horse so that the takeoff and hand contact on the horse *cannot* occur simultaneously.
4. At takeoff from the board, shift eye focus upward (overhead) and reach for that spot before looking at the horse.
5. Just after takeoff from the board (on vertical lift), tighten the entire body, especially hips and legs, and lift heels overhead.

TEACHING AIDS

1. Practice handstand snap downs to squat, straddle, and stoop stand to assist in learning the action of legs and hips in the layout vaults.
2. Practice swan jump from board; spotter stands in front of the board to catch the performer at waist area. This will help develop vertical lift and also help get the feeling of flying.
3. Spring into swan dive from the minitramp onto the trampoline.
4. Practice hitting layout position and landing on stack of mats in a squat position.
5. Practice hitting layout and landing in squat on trampoline.
6. Practice layout dive rolls landing on crash pad.
7. Using reuther board and side horse at regulation height; use spotters on near side of horse to help lift performer to proper position.
8. Hang a jump rope (or rope of another type with some kind of weight at the end) over pegs of a high jump standard and have students vault over the rope before making contact with the horse. Make sure rope will move easily so performer will not fall if her feet catch on the rope.
9. If an overhead spotting system is available, put students in belt and help them perform handspring and cartwheel vaults.

LAYOUT VAULTS (Fig. 305)

Since the layout vaults have many common errors that are the same, the following list will be referred to for all vaults; errors peculiar to each vault will be listed under the performance technique of that vault.

Figure 305

General common errors

1. Insufficient run, hurdle, and takeoff from the board.
2. Leaning forward on takeoff from the board.
3. Piking on preflight (failure to tighten gluteal, thigh, and back muscles after takeoff from the board).
4. Failure to attain layout position before executing the desired vault.
   a. Below horizontal.
   b. Barely horizontal.
   c. Slightly above horizontal.
   Layout position should be at least at a 45° angle.
5. Failure to place hands on *top* of horse.
6. Allowing arms to bend.
7. Allowing legs to bend (except in squat vault).
8. Landing heavy on the horse with hands.
9. Failure to push off the horse with the hands immediately after contact. If hands remain on horse too long, usually the afterflight will be slow and low.
10. Allowing shoulders to be forward of hand position on the horse.
11. Allowing shoulders to shrug as hands contact horse.
12. Allowing feet to touch the horse during any part of the vault.
13. Insufficient afterflight (must be upward as well as outward).
14. Failure to keep head up and back and to lift upper body for proper direction on the afterflight.
15. Failure to extend body fully before landing.
16. Failure to land lightly and with control.

Layout squat (Fig. 306).

Figure 306

PT After attaining a layout position from the vertical lift, tuck knees to chest. Push off of the horse with hands while simultaneously lifting head and chest. As body passes over the horse, force hips forward to extend body before landing. Focus eyes on the board before running, upward before takeoff on board, on the horse on preflight, and foreupward on the afterflight. Slightly flex knees and hips upon landing. After push off from the horse arms go foreupward, then obliquely forward upon landing.

SP Use as many as four spotters, two on near side of horse and two on far side. Spotters on near side help performer attain layout position by placing one hand on her thigh and other on her abdomen. Spotters on far side of horse beside performer help lift and pull performer over the horse by grasping her upper arms. Maintain contact until balanced landing is achieved.

Layout stoop (Fig. 307)

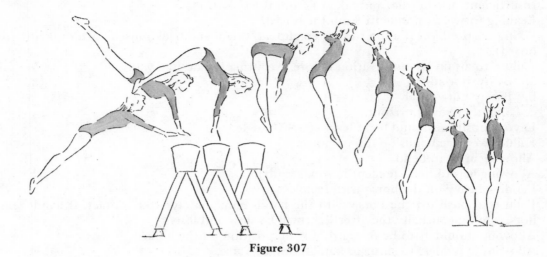

Figure 307

PT   After attaining a layout position from the vertical lift and contacting the horse with hands, forcefully flex hips and drive legs through arms (without bending knees). Push off of the horse with hands while simultaneously lifting head and upper body. Force hips forward to completely extend body before landing. Eye focus and arm action is the same as for the layout squat.

SP   Same as for the layout squat vault.

Layout straddle (Fig. 308)

Figure 308

PT   After attaining a layout position from the vertical lift and contacting the horse with hands, move legs to a wide straddle position. Push off the horse with hands while simultaneously lifting head and upper body. As body passes over the horse, keep hips forward and bring legs together before landing. (Many beginners tend to flex hips after straddle position is attained and then force legs forward. This will decrease their afterflight and means that they must make an extra hip movement since the body must be fully extended before landing.)

CE Allowing legs to straddle before layout position is achieved.

SP Stand on far side of horse in front of performer. As performer places hands on horse, grasp upper arms and help pull and lift (if necessary) her over the horse. Maintain contact until balance is achieved. Have one foot in front of the other so that you can step back as the performer clears the horse so that she can have some afterflight.

HANDSPRING VAULT (Fig. 309)

Figure 309

PT During vertical lift reach more upward with arms than for a layout vault so that the flight of the body can be more up then onto the horse for continual motion over the horse. The body should be in an inverted position when contact (of hands) is made on the horse. Head must be between arms. As hands contact the horse, shoulders give very slightly so that hands and shoulders can extend forcefully to push body upward, then outward. The body must remain in an arched position until landing. Arms must remain overhead during the afterflight, and head should remain up. Toes should reach out toward the mat and, as they contact the mat, knees and hips flex slightly and arms move to a back oblique position.

SP 1. Two spotters on near side of horse spot same as for layout vault. Two spotters on far side of horse grasp upper arms with inside hands and lower back with outside hands.
2. Spotter on near side of horse in front of performer between the reuther board and the horse. As the performer takes off from the board, place hands on waist and hip area and assist her to handstand position. As contact is made with the performer, the spotter should bend knees and lift with legs rather than straining the arms and back. Spotter on the far side of the horse grasps upper arm and small of back as for technique above.

CE 1. 1—3 and 5—16 of the general common errors for layout vaulting.
2. Failure to make arm lift high and then onto horse.
3. Failure to reach inverted position as hands contact horse.
4. Allowing the shoulders to sag when hands contact horse.
5. Failure to keep arms overhead, head up and back, and body arched on the afterflight.

GIANT CARTWHEEL (Fig. 310)

Figure 310

PT   After takeoff from the board make quarter (90°) turn with entire body. As the first hand contacts the horse, the body should be almost in an inverted position. As the second hand contacts the horse, lift the first hand. Keep body straight and sideward in the afterflight, with feet pointing toward the direction of the vault.

SP   Same as for handspring vault.

CE   1.   Same as 1—3 and 5—16 of general common errors for layout vaults.
       2.   Turning too soon or too late.
       3.   Failure to maintain a sideways position (after turn is made) throughout skill.

HECHT (Fig. 311)

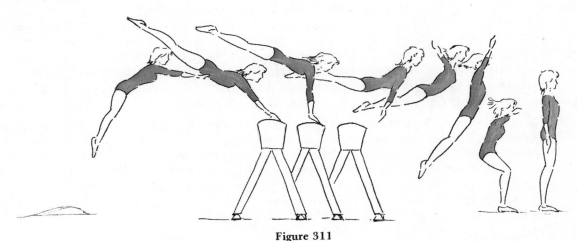

Figure 311

PT   Take a fast run and hurdle. Upon contacting the board, lean forward, keeping eyes focused on the middle of the horse. Keep head close to arms as they reach for the horse. As hands contact the horse, arms should be almost in line with upper body. The entire body should be horizontal, with hips slightly flexed. The head and shoulders should follow through with the downward thrust created with the hand push-off from the horse. (This action usually raises the hips and will in turn elevate the entire body.) As body is almost over the horse, raise arms slightly, and arch back slightly; keep the eyes focused on the landing area. Flex hips and allow legs to be brought under body; try to delay knee bend until feet contact the mat.

SP   Stand on far side of horse. As performer passes over horse, place inside hand on lower back and outside hand on abdomen to help lift her forward, then upward. Two spotters should be used. Maintain contact until landing.

CE   1. Insufficient run.
      2. Insufficient forward lean on takeoff from the board.
      3. Failure to keep head between arms as hands contact horse.
      4. Failure to allow body to follow the downward movement from the hand push-off.
      5. Failure to have shoulders slightly behind hands on horse contact.
      6. Failure to slightly arch back and flex hips to land.
      7. Bending knees before feet contact mat.

YAMASHITA (Fig. 312)

Figure 312

PT   Begin front handspring vault. As body reaches the inverted position on the horse and push-off is about to occur, forcefully flex hips and upper body to bring body to a tight piked position. Immediately extend hips, forcing legs upward and outward while entire body is moving upward and outward in an arched position. Continue reaching for the mat with toes and slightly flex hips and knees upon landing. Eyes spot knees when going into piked position, object overhead when returning to arched position, and then object at eye level upon landing.

SP   Same as for front handspring. Be careful not to inhibit piking action of performer by spotting too closely.

CE   1. Same as for handspring vault.
      2. Insufficient pike.
      3. Piking too soon or too late.
      4. Failure to extend legs upward as well as outward after piking.
      5. Slow action getting into and out of piked position.
      6. Failure to return to an arched position before landing.

NOTES

CHAPTER SEVEN
TRAMPOLINE

The trampoline is a very versatile piece of equipment and should be used in all gymnastic curriculums. Because of its size, it can present problems when trying to arrange all the equipment in a small area. If this is your particular situation, possibly a unit for tumbling, mini-tramp, and trampoline can be taught for a couple of weeks, then bars, beam, and vaulting.

The skills to be covered are as follows:

Basic bounce

Killing the bounce (stopping)

Tuck jump

Straddle jump

Half turn

Seat drop

Knee drop

Roll over (seat drop—full twist—seat drop)

Full turn

Swivel hips

Back drop

Cradle

Front flip

Back flip

Baroni

Front sommie with half twist

Layout

Full twisting layout

Other uses of the trampoline are suggested at the end of the chapter.

Safety Precautions

1. Never leave the trampoline unsupervised.
2. Teach students how to properly fold and unfold the trampoline.
3. Replace strings or shock cords when damaged.
4. Have mats on dismount end of trampoline.

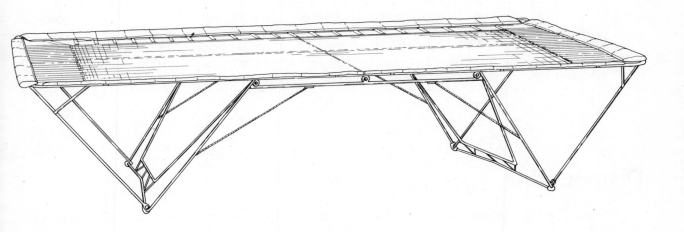

5. Never allow students to bounce alone.
6. Have alert spotters—spotters should know what skills are being performed.
7. Bounce in the middle of the trampoline (unless doing doubles bouncing).
8. When tired, stop bouncing—individuals should bounce for short periods of time.
9. When dizzy, stop bouncing.
10. Perform skills at own level—do not attempt new skills without proper instruction.

Spotting Techniques

1. The basic skills can be learned from a low bounce. As the performer gains confidence, she may attempt the skills from a higher bounce.
2. For some of the intermediate and advanced skills, hand spotting may be used. The spotter must bounce *with* the performer—at a designated count (usually three) the spotter must flex his or her knees, stay on the bed of the trampoline and manually rotate the performer.
3. When using an overhead spotting belt, first make sure the ropes attached to the belt are even and fairly tight. (Pull down on the ropes to take up the slack as the performer bounces up.) When the performer is ready to do the skill (usually on a designated count), the spotter pulls very hard on the ropes so the student may complete the skill in the air.

SPOTTING BELTS

There are two types of spotting belts. One is usually a plain canvas strap very much like a regular belt. The second type of belt is a twisting belt which has a regular belt attached to an outside metal frame. The latter allows the performer to twist freely in the air without getting caught in the ropes.

Mounting the Trampoline

1. Jump to a sitting position.
   a. Stand facing the trampoline. Place hands on the frame. Jump up and turn to sit on frame.
   b. Stand with back to frame—jump up to sitting position.
2. For small children, have some type of sturdy steps or lift them onto the trampoline. NEVER USE FOLDING CHAIRS.
3. When children reach the intermediate level, they could mount with a forward roll—being careful to keep head from between springs. If students have used the mini-tramp, they could mount by rebounding off the mini-tramp into a dive roll onto the trampoline.

Dismounting

1. Crawl, scoot, or walk slowly to the end of the tramp. Sit down and hop off onto designated mat.
2. In advanced classes a front flip or Barani may be used as a dismount.

Basic Skills

It is important to understand that all skills are initiated from the bed of the tramp even though the actual movement is completed in the air. To prove this to students have one on the tramp bouncing. As her feet leave the bed immediately give her a command to do a seat drop or half turn or some other skill. Make sure she does not know what skill will be called. She will find herself unable to do this skill unless she takes another bounce. Sometimes advanced performers can defeat this theory with beginning skills because of the great amount of control and height they have developed in their bounce. In order to show various positions of the body in a skill we have made it look like the skill starts in one place on the tramp and finishes in another. Most skills, however, are performed in the same vertical or horizontal plane.

BASIC BOUNCE (Fig. 313)

Figure 313

PT *Legs*—Start with feet shoulder width apart. Bend knees and jump by extending legs and ankles completely. Toes should be pointing toward the bed while the body is suspended in air. When landing, toes contact the bed first, immediately followed by the feet. Ankles and knees flex slightly to prepare for the next lift upward.

Note: After students feel comfortable bouncing, they should bring the legs together while in the air.

Arms—Two basic arm movements are used.
1. Circular—arm movement is similar to the arm pattern of the breast stroke. Start with arms sideways but forward, with elbows slightly bent. As knees bend to begin the upward jump, arms go down and together in front of the body. As the body projects upward the arms go to an overhead position assisting with the lift.

   Arms should never be allowed to go behind the body, as this tends to throw the body off balance.
2. Up-down oblique—arms move from a downward position to an upward oblique position when the body is in the air. There is no circular motion in this technique.

Eye Focus—Depending on the individual, students should:
1. focus on subject at eye level;
2. focus on frame of tramp;
3. use no focus.

CE 1. Bouncing flat footed—not completely extending the ankles.
2. Bending knees too much when contacting bed.
3. Allowing arms to move behind body.
4. Improper coordination of arms and legs.
5. Letting eyes wander, turning the head, or looking down at bed of tramp.

KILLING THE BOUNCE (Stopping) (Fig. 314)

Figure 314

PT When contacting the bed of the tramp, quickly flex the knees and hips as if to sit and move arms forward in front of the body.

TUCK JUMP (Fig. 315)

Figure 315

PT As the body approaches the peak of the bounce, lift knees to chest. As body begins downward movement extend the legs before contacting the tramp bed. Arms may touch knees or ankles while in tuck position.

CE 1. Leaning forward while in tuck position.
2. Insufficient tuck.

STRADDLE JUMP (Fig. 316)

PT Just before reaching the peak of the bounce lift the legs high and wide in a straddle position. Keep upper body straight and touch toes with hands.

CE Beginners tend to lower the upper body forward rather than lifting the legs upward.

Figure 316

HALF TURN (Fig. 317) (Should be practiced right and left)

Figure 317

PT Initiate turn from bounce upward and continue to turn after feet leave the bed. The turn should be completed at the peak of the bounce. The head should be turned in the direction of the turn. The arms may be at the side of the body, in the air, or one in the air with the other pulling across the body in the direction of the turn.

CE Not turning the head in the direction of the turn.

SEAT DROP (Fig. 318)

Figure 318

POB (Position on bed) Open pike position. Legs together and straight—toes pointed. Upper body erect and hands placed by the hips on the bed of the tramp, with fingers pointing toward toes.

PT As body is reaching peak of bounce, lift legs so they are parallel to the bed. Allow upper body to tilt back ever so slightly. Remain in this position until contacting tramp. Push with hands on tramp; then lift overhead to assist in bringing body to upright position.

CE 1. Not lifting legs high enough, causing heels to hit tramp before rest of body.
2. Lifting legs too high, causing performer to land on buttocks and back.
3. Not keeping legs straight upon contact with tramp. When legs are bent it is more difficult to return to a standing position.

VA 1. Seat drop with legs in a straddle position.
2. Half turn into seat drop.
3. Tuck or straddle jump into seat drop.

KNEE DROP (Fig. 319)

Figure 319

POB Body erect from knees up. Legs bent at knees, with knees to ankle in contact with tramp. Toes pointed to prevent injury. Arms slightly forward and at waist level ready to assist in upward movement.

PT As the body is reaching the peak of the bounce, bend legs, keeping upper body erect. After contact is made in this position, use arms to assist in lifting body to standing position.

CE 1. Sitting back on heels on tramp.
2. Lifting heels too high—lower leg should be parallel to bed.

Combination
1. Seat drop, knee drop, seat drop.
2. Half turn, knee drop.

ROLL-OVER or SEAT DROP, FULL TWIST, SEAT DROP (Fig. 320)

Figure 320

PT From a seat drop, push forcefully with the hands on the tramp. As the body moves upward, allow the upper body to drop backward so the body is almost horizontal to the tramp (in the air). Pull the left arm forcefully across the chest and face to assist with the full turn. As the turn is completed, drop the hips backward and downward and bring the upper body forward so as to land in seat drop position.

Note: During the twisting move, keep hips and legs as tight as possible.

CE 1. Trying to twist out of a poorly executed seat drop.
2. Trying to twist while in the sitting position.
3. Twisting too soon or too late.
4. Not dropping the turning shoulder directly toward tramp bed where seat drop was performed.

FULL TURN (Fig. 321)

Figure 321

PT As the body is reaching the peak of the bounce, force the outside arm across the body toward the direction of the turn. Look in the direction of the turn. Complete the full turn before landing.

Note: Some people can turn easily and, therefore, do not need the force from the opposite arm. Arms can be at sides for these individuals.

CE 1. Turning too soon or too late.
2. Completely relaxing the body during the turn. The body should be completely vertical and as tight as possible.
3. Turning in the wrong direction—if an individual is not successful turning to the right, have her turn to the left and vice versa.
4. Looking in the opposite direction of the turn.

SWIVEL HIPS (Fig. 322) Seat drop, half turn, seat drop

Figure 322

PT From a seat drop completely extend the body to a vertical position with arms overhead. Make a half turn looking in the direction of the turn; then flex the hips and go into another seat drop.

CE Failure to push with the hands and *to extend the body fully before turning and sitting*.

Lead-up: Seat drop—stand in air and reach for ceiling.
Seat drop—vertical position, half turn.
Seat drop—half turn half seat drop.

BACK DROP (Fig. 323)

Figure 323

POB Body in piked position; hips raised from bed; landing is on middle to upper back; chin tucked toward chest with arms by knees.

PT To learn a back drop, hold the arms in front of body as if holding a ball. Lift one leg as if to kick ball, followed by other. Land in piked position on back with chin tucked. The action necessary to get the body back to a standing position is the same as that used in a kip on the floor (except for arms). The legs shoot upward and outward at a 45° angle; hips are forced upward and forward and upper body is arched, with head slightly back and arms overhead.

CE 1. Not keeping head tucked when hitting backdrop position.
2. Landing on buttocks or shoulder area rather than back.
3. Not using force from legs and hips to return to standing position.
4. Not taking advantage of spring from trampoline to push body upward.

CRADLE (Back drop half turn back drop)

PT When the body is returning upward from a backdrop, the legs and hips are extended. As the body reaches its peak, rotate hips and shoulders 180°, pike body again, and land on back facing opposite direction. Then extend body to standing position.

Lead-up: *Back drop with half twist to stand* (Fig. 324)

Figure 324

Note: For those girls who have worked an underswing half turn on unevens, you can compare body actions from back drop to half turn to the compressed position to the extended position.

Another hint might be to do a back drop, come forward as if to do a front drop, half turn to back drop.

CE 1. Poor back drop.
2. Extending too soon—wait until body is in air before twisting.
3. Twisting too late—usually results in landing on side.

FRONT FLIP (Fig. 325) Front sommie

Figure 325

PT As the body is reaching the peak of the bounce, with arms overhead raise the hips forcefully backupward; force arms downward, tuck head, bring knees to chest, and rotate 360°. Just before the feet come under the body, extend legs, chest, and head so as to land on feet in standing position.

Lead-up:
1. Knee drop forward spin to back. MAKE SURE STUDENTS GO UP OUT OF KNEE DROP BEFORE SPINNING. LETTING THEM TURN FORWARD FROM THE BED ONLY CREATES BAD HABITS AND, OF COURSE, POOR TECHNIQUE.
2. Knee drop forward spin to seat.
3. Knee drop forward spin to feet.
4. Regular low bounce to back.
5. Regular low bounce to seat.
6. Regular low bounce to feet.

CE 1. Turning forward from bed rather than waiting until body is in air.
2. Closing eyes.
3. Not tucking tightly enough.
4. Turning head to side while rotating.
5. Using one arm more than the other. (4 and 5 cause spin to be crooked.)
6. Not opening soon enough.

VA *Front flip in piked position* (Fig. 326)

Figure 326

BACK SOMMIE (Fig. 327a)

Figure 327a

PT As the peak of the bounce is reached, with arms overhead forcefully lift knees to chest, keeping head in normal position. Complete spin in air. After the back and head have passed the horizontal position (three-quarters of the skill has been completed and the back is to the ceiling), extend legs and come to standing position.

CE 1. Starting the rotation too soon.
2. *Whipping the head back.*
3. Turning the head to one side, thus causing an oblique rotation.
4. Not opening the tuck soon enough.

SP 1. Spot with overhead belt.
2. Hand spot—one hand on back of upper leg, other on small of back (Fig. 327b). On designated count (usually three) stay on bed of trampoline and lift and rotate body with hand on leg, and support, then rotate with hand on back.

Figure 327b

VA *Back sommie in piked position* (Fig. 328)

Figure 328

BARANI (Fig. 329)

Figure 329

PT The easiest way to describe this move is that it is very similar to a round-off. As the peak of the bounce is reached, the hips thrust backupward and the body moves forward as if to do a front sommie. THE EYES FOCUS ON THE MIDDLE OF THE TRAMPOLINE AT ALL TIMES FROM THIS POINT. The lower body rotates over the head making a half turn. The hips flex at this point to come to a standing position.

CE 1. Not focusing eyes on the bed of tramp throughout skill.
2. Starting the skill too soon—wait until body is in the air.
3. Directing hips and legs around rather than directly over head.

SP Use overhead gear with twisting belt.

FRONT SOMMIE WITH HALF TWIST (Fig. 330)

Figure 330

PT Start the same as for a front sommie in piked position. Continue until the body has almost reached an inverted piked position. Eyes focus on knees. At this point extend hips so that legs move through L position. At this point start looking in the direction of the turn. When the body has made the half twist, it will be horizontal to the tramp. Flex the hips and lift the upper body to come to a standing position.

CE 1. Not completing three-quarters of the front sommie before beginning the twist.
2. Not looking in the direction of the turn.
3. Looking in one direction and trying to force the arms in another.
4. Not using arms to start rotary motion.

SP Use overhead gear with twisting belt.

LAYOUT (Fig. 331)

PT As the body leaves the bed of the tramp completely tighten all muscles, especially the hips. Keep head in normal position and lift forcefully with chest, and body will rotate around head to land on feet.

Figure 331

CE 1. Whipping head back as body leaves tramp.
2. Not staying taut or tight in hip area throughout move.
3. Not concentrating on a lift with the chest.

SP 1. Use overhead spotting gear with regular belt.
2. Hand spot—on designated count (usually "three") stay on bed of tramp, flex knees while placing one hand on hip, one on lower back. Lift and rotate hip area clockwise.

Figure 332

PT Use same takeoff as for layout. Turn the head and shoulder in the direction of the twist and look at the hip area. Pull outside arm across body. Body will continue twisting as it rotates around head. As the body reaches the vertical position, focus eyes on bed of trampoline, and keep them focused there until twist is finished. Flex hips slightly and slightly lift head to come to a standing position.

CE 1. Not keeping body straight and tight throughout entire skill.
2. Twisting too soon (start layout first).
3. Twisting too late.
4. Not using arms for assisting in the turning action of the body.

SP Use overhead gear with a twisting belt.

Other Uses for the Trampoline

The trampoline can be used for a number of tasks. One of the main reasons for using the trampoline for learning tumbling and vaulting skills is to save wear and tear on the legs and feet. It also helps avoid shin splints and, of course, on some skills eliminates the fear of falling on a hard surface. The following are just a few suggested uses for the trampoline; use your imagination!

TRAMPOLINE AS AN EXERCISE BARRE (Fig. 333 - 335)

Depending on the exercises to be done, a large number of girls can work around the trampoline doing leg lifts (Fig. 333), stretching exercises (Fig. 334), or working on body positions such as the arabesque and grand battement (Fig. 335).

Figure 333

Figure 334

Figure 335

TRAMPOLINE AS A TUMBLING AID (Fig. 336 - 337)

Figure 336

The skills shown below are just some of many that can be learned on the trampoline. Even in beginning tumbling when an individual is having difficulty rolling over on a backward roll, the trampoline can be used to show poor technique. In advanced tumbling it is especially helpful to learn skills such as the front and back sommies, layouts, and twisting moves on the trampoline first. These skills are a bit easier to spot on a trampoline and, of course, landing on the trampoline is much easier on the feet and legs than landing on mats. The back handspring (Fig. 336) learned on the trampoline does not offer the performer a true feeling of the skill, so after learning in the middle of the tramp the student can stand on the frame of the tramp (which better assimilates the push action on the floor) and perform the skill onto the bed of the trampoline (Fig. 337).

Figure 337

TRAMPOLINE AS A VAULTING AID (Fig. 338 - 341)

Because the trampoline is approximately the same height as a horse, it can easily be used to learn and practice many vaulting skills. Two safety rules should always be enforced when using the trampoline for vaulting: (1) a mat should be draped over the end of the trampoline so no one falls through the shock cords or springs and (2) someone should always be at the opposite end and sides to assist if a student should lose her balance upon landing. When performing handspring or yamishita vaults on the trampoline, it is sometimes helpful to have a crash pad on top of the bed of the trampoline to absorb some of the spring. The following figures show the use of the trampoline for practicing and learning beginning through advanced vaults.

Figure 338

Figure 339

Figure 340

Figure 341

USE OF TRAMPOLINE FOR LEARNING BEAM DISMOUNTS (Fig. 342 - 343)

When using the beam for learning certain dismounts such as shown below, place the side or end of beam over the trampoline. Some beams may have to be raised slightly for a nice fit. When attempting the back (Fig. 342) or front (Fig. 343) flip dismount onto the trampoline, make sure a spotter is standing close enough to assist if balance is lost.

Figure 342

Figure 343

TRAMPOLINE FOR LEARNING SOME UNEVEN BAR SKILLS (Fig. 344)

Because of its design, the trampoline is not really very helpful in learning many uneven bar skills. However, some skills such as the cast away (Fig. 344) or squat stand can be learned on the frame.

Figure 344

The above are just a few uses for the versatile piece of equipment called the trampoline. Put your mind to work and you will be able to come up with some very unique uses.

NOTES

NOTES

CHAPTER EIGHT
CLASS ORGANIZATION

"What on earth am I going to do with fifty students in half a gym during the gymnastic unit?" This question is often asked by teachers confronted with the same or similar situation. It is hoped that the following suggestions can be used or varied to fit your particular needs and that they will, to some extent, offer a solution to the question above.

Planning ahead seems to be the key to success. Check to see what equipment you have, what equipment you need, and the amount of money available for purchasing equipment and supplies.

It is most likely that all apparatus cannot be purchased at one time, so the following is suggested:

1. First check into those dark corners of the equipment room; you can usually find a horse or a set of parallel bars. If there are no parallel bars, look for a horizontal bar; and even if your school has the "wall flower" type, it can be put to good use.
2. Check the mats. Do you have an adequate number? Are they in good condition? Remember that you need mats to surround the apparatus as well as for tumbling.
3. Since you can use the parallel bars (by removing one bar) or the horizontal bar for learning beginning skills for the uneven parallel bar, I would suggest ordering a balance beam (one that adjusts to a low, medium, and regulation height) and a reuther board.

CHAOS

4. If no equipment is available, the following purchase order would be suggested: Mats, beam, uneven parallel bars (plus extra bar), reuther board, horse, and trampoline. Some type of transporter should also be ordered so that equipment can be moved easily and safely.

Supplies such as magnesium (chalk), chalk stands, resin, colored tape (for marking areas on mat and apparatus), spotting belts, and other safety aids, such as a beam pad, should be ordered with the equipment.

Secure information on available films (for rental and purchase), wall charts, and bulletin board material. Some of the visual aids materials can be obtained free of charge from the apparatus distributors.

Check the school library and your personal library and make a list of reference books. Order books and magazines if necessary.

Equipment

ORDERING EQUIPMENT

Ordering equipment is not an easy task. Teachers or administrators should first investigate what is presently on the market, then use the following criteria as a guideline for purchasing the equipment.

1. What safety features does the apparatus have?
2. Is the apparatus durable? Does the apparatus have a guarantee?
3. Is the apparatus adaptable to your needs?
4. Is the apparatus easily moved from place to place? Can it be stored without too much difficulty?
5. Does the apparatus meet FIG specifications? (If the apparatus is to be used at any time for competition, it is essential that it be adjustable to proper heights etc.)
6. *Will the company service the apparatus promptly and efficiently?*
7. The least important factor should be the cost of the equipment. Usually if a little more is paid for the equipment initially, chances are that it will not have to be serviced or replaced frequently.

To secure information on apparatus, obtain catalogues from district salesmen, write directly to the company, or pick up some catalogues at professional convention exhibitions. It is also advisable to discuss this matter with colleagues who have used various makes of apparatus before making a final decision.

The five major companies supplying gymnastic equipment are (in alphabetical order):

1. American Athletic Equipment
   Jefferson, Iowa 50129

2. Gym Master Company
   3200 South Zuni Street
   Englewood, Colorado 80110

3. Nissen Corporation
   930 27th Avenue S.W.
   Cedar Rapids, Iowa 52406

4. Porter Athletic Equipment
   9555 West Irving Park Road
   Schiller Park, Illinois 60176

5. Program Aids Co., Inc.
   550 Garden Avenue
   Mt. Vernon, New York 10553

CARE OF EQUIPMENT

Since gymnastic equipment is expensive initially, special care should be taken to keep it in good condition for as long as possible. If maintenance is performed, equipment can last indefinitely.

1. Check equipment before each use (refer to chapters on apparatus for details).
2. Have adequate number of students moving equipment so they do not injure themselves or damage the equipment.

3. Wash mats to clean off chalk dust, dirt, or body oils.
4. Make sure equipment is properly used; do not let balance beam be used as a clothes rack or a seat for twenty students.
5. Before each unit or once a year have a representative from the company from which the equipment was purchased (or other personnel with proper knowledge of the equipment) examine the apparatus to make certain it is in top usable condition.

Now About Those Fifty Students!

Of course, one of the best ways to handle large groups in any situation is to have assistants. One of the following may be a solution for your particular problem.
1. Train girls to spot (before or after school).
2. Limit the number of skills required in the unit.
3. Use a buddy system.
4. Give a good basic course for all students, and start an after school club or team for advanced or interested students.

WAYS TO ORGANIZE STUDENTS WITHIN GROUPS

1. Ability grouping: beginners, intermediates, and advanced. Have a progression for each group.
2. Buddy system: pair a weak individual with a strong individual or have an advanced student with a beginner student.
3. Somatotype the students: have three groups—one of mesomorphs, one of endomorphs, and one of ectomorphs. Refer to glossary for definition of terms. Definitions are for extreme somatotypes; however, individuals are usually combinations of these various body structures.
4. Random grouping: first six in group one, second six in group two, etc.

WAYS TO ORGANIZE LARGE GROUPS IN EACH AREA OF GYMNASTICS

TUMBLING

1. Use cross-mat tumbling technique.
   a. Number off by fours and have every fourth girl perform at one time with the person to the left acting as the spotter.
   b. File students: after one girl has almost finished performing the second starts, etc.
   c. After students can perform skills well, give commands and have every other student perform.

   Example: Forward Roll commands—Step onto mat, squat, place hands on mat, roll.

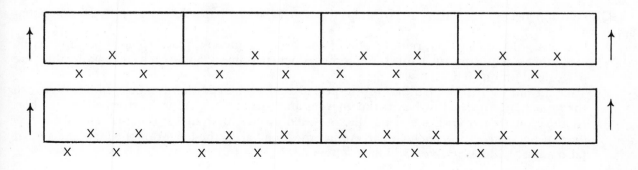

2. Arrange mats in semi-circle.
   a. Apply same techniques as above or work in groups of four if mats are of adequate size.
   b. Allow students to work in these groups at their own pace with two performing and the other two acting as spotters.

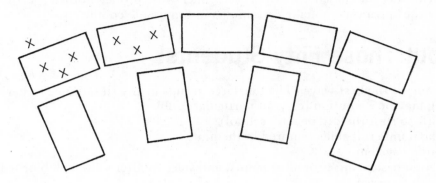

FLOOR EXERCISE

For large groups it is almost always impossible to have students perform individual routines due to limited time and space. You can revert to a mass exercise made up either in advance or created during one or two class sessions, with the students helping design the routine and floor pattern. Refer to floor exercise chapter for more suggestions.

A floor exercise mat can be made by covering carpet padding with a large piece of canvas.

BALANCE BEAM

It is not likely that any school will have ten balance beams, so teachers must make use of improvised equipment. The following suggestions might benefit your particular situation.
1. Most gymnasiums have lines for basketball and volleyball courts. These lines can be utilized by the students to practice skills before attempting them on the beam.
2. Some gyms have stages. If yours has, use the stage as a partial beam. Even though this is a one-sided arrangement, students can get the feeling of being off the floor to some degree. Depending on the height of the stage, mounts can also be practiced here.
3. Possibly the industrial arts department in your school would agree to make a couple of low beams. This is a very inexpensive task.
4. If the gym has bleachers, use the first row as a low beam.

UNEVEN PARALLEL BARS

Girls do not need a regulation set of uneven parallel bars to begin learning skills suited to that apparatus.
1. Use a set of parallel bars; remove one of the bars completely, place some type of covering over the open support (towel or some other padding), and teach the skills that are performed on one bar.
2. Take advantage of the high bar also, especially the wall type that is adjustable. Lower it to the same height as the low bar of the unevens and work skills that are performed on one bar.
3. Remove one bar from a set of parallel bars. Adjust height so that it is equivalent to the low uneven bar; move it to the high bar. Adjust the high bar to the height of the high uneven bar (also adjust width), and you will have a homemade set of uneven parallel bars.

VAULTING

Playing leap frog is probably the most elementary form of vaulting. (Many students enjoy reverting back to their childhood games.) This activity could be used as a lead-up. If vaulting equipment is not available, the following substitutes can be used.

1. Vault over the balance beam at medium height. Cover the beam with mats. More than one girl can vault simultaneously, but avoid vaulting near the supports.
2. *Very stable* benches or narrow tables covered with mats can also be used for vaulting.
3. Mats rolled up, as long as they are not too wide, can be used.

General Safety Factors

1. Make sure apparatus is in good condition and properly mantled.
2. Have adequate mats surrounding the equipment.
3. Arrange apparatus so that students can work without fear of falling into or onto another object.
4. Have students in proper physical condition before allowing them to work on the apparatus. (See suggested exercises.)
5. Allow students to rest when fatigued.
6. Keep interest up by varying exercises or skills on apparatus and not making requirements too difficult.
7. Teach good spotting techniques as well as mechanical techniques.
8. Make sure the area is well lit and properly ventilated.
9. Teach with a positive approach to avoid developing fear in students.
10. Have a definite skill progression for each class.

Spotting

Spotting is in itself an art. It is not always putting a student through an entire skill but rather giving assistance where most needed for success and to prevent injury. Spotting can be done with hand contact, mechanical devices (e.g., spotting belt), or just readiness to assist if necessary. The last method is mainly used in competition.

In all spotting work, it is the duty of the spotter to prevent the head from falling to the mat or striking any part of the apparatus. Therefore, the most common points of contact for spotting are the performer's shoulder, upper arm, back, and wrist.

In general, the spotter should stand close to the apparatus and should understand that she must sacrifice her own safety to assist the performer. Except for an occasional slap on the face with an uncontrolled hand, a spotter is seldom hurt.

The spotter should know the following about the skill she is spotting.

1. Position of the body from the beginning throughout the entire skill.
2. What part of the body produces the force or momentum to initiate movement of the skill.
3. What parts of the body control the movement of the skill, such as the hands, hips, feet, etc.
4. In what part(s) of the skill are accidents most likely to occur, and what can be done to prevent accidents or to assist the performer at that point.

Remember that giving proper assistance to women in gymnastic skills is of utmost importance in maintaining their interest and in creating confidence in you as a spotter. Always be alert.

Know what to expect from your students. Have a definite skill progression and do not allow them to attempt advanced skills before they have mastered the basic skills. If there are lead-ups to skills and if the student cannot perform them, she should not be allowed to attempt the skill itself.

It might be advisable to post a chart with the skill progressions to make students aware of the necessity for learning in this particular manner.

Methods for Testing

SUBJECTIVE EVALUATION

1. Each skill can be analyzed and parts charted for testing. This is the most objective type of evaluation, but it is not feasible in large classes.
   Example: Forward Roll
   _____ Squat—knees together.
   _____ Hands in front of body on mat.
   _____ Extended legs, pushing equally with both feet.
   _____ Bent arms and tucked head at proper time.
   _____ No loud sound when rolling onto back.
   _____ Legs together and straight when inverted.
   _____ Legs tucked at proper time.
   _____ Stand executed without loss of balance and without using hand to push to stand.
2. Rate skill as whole (0 to 4 points)
   0 (F) Failed to perform skill.
   1 (D) Performance—some phases correct, some incorrect, poor form.
   2 (C) Performance—mechanics correct, poor form, skill not performed smoothly.
   3 (B) Performance—mechanically correct, form good.
   4 (A) Performance—mechanically correct with very good form and control.
3. Pass or fail grading system
   1. Failure—unable to perform skill.
   2. Pass—able to perform skill whether mechanically correct or not and with either good or poor form.

OBJECTIVE EVALUATION IN GYMNASTICS

Evaluation in physical education should not be on skill alone. There are many students who can understand and analyse movement very well but can not perform as efficiently as others. With these students, we should try to encourage those more physically gifted to be able to understand and apply principles of movement when performing to obtain maximum results. We should not only teach the "how," but also the "why," "when," and "relationship of this movement to another."

The following are examples of test questions that can be used at the secondary (junior and senior high) level and college level (for physical education majors).

JUNIOR—SENIOR HIGH

Tumbling
1. When performing a forward roll, where are the hands placed?
   a. Between the legs on the mat
   b. Forward of the knees on the mat
   c. To the side of the knees on the mat
   d. It doesn't make any difference where the hands are placed
2. In performing the forward roll, when is the head tucked toward the chest?
   a. When the hands are placed on the mat
   b. Before the hands are placed on the mat
   c. As the hips are raised and the legs extend
   d. As the elbows bend
3. When spotting tumbling skills, our main concern is protection of what part of the body?
   a. Head
   b. Eyes
   c. Back
   d. Arms

Balance Beam

1. When working on the balance beam it is important that we have an _____ spotter.
   a. Friendly
   b. Strong
   c. Alert
   d. Passive
2. On the beam we use which of the following types of walks?
   a. Flat-footed
   b. Dance
   c. Ordinary
   d. Fast
3. List three classifications of skills we learned on the beam. (Answers will depend on what teacher covered in class.)
   1. Rolls
   2. Locomotor skills
   3. Poses
   4. Dance moves
   5. Mounts
   6. Dismounts

Uneven Bars

1. List three grips used on the unevens and beside it a skill that requires the use of that grip. Example of answers
GRIP	SKILL
a. Forward	a. Back hip circle
2. Proper body position in the front support position involves all but which one of the following?
   a. Shoulders hunched
   b. Upper thighs on bar
   c. Arms straight
   d. Legs straight and together
3. It is important to learn the cast (push-away) well so that we can perform other skills. Which of the following skills is not preceeded by a cast?
   a. Back hip circle
   b. Single leg shoot through
   c. Double leg shoot through
   d. Back hip pull over

Vaulting

1. The side of the horse closest to the reuther board is referred to as the (near) side.
2. In order to perform a good vault, the run must be executed in which of the following manners?
   a. Sluggish
   b. Fast all the way
   c. Slow, then fast before the hurdle
   d. Slow, but with a long stride
3. The spotter for a squat vault should be on the far side of the horse and do which of the following?
   a. Grab shoulder of performer and pull her over the horse
   b. Grasp upper arm and assist in lifting performer up and over the horse
   c. Assist only if performer needs help
   d. None of the above

Floor Exercise

1. The time limit of a competitive routine is (60) to (90) seconds.
2. List three components of a floor exercise routine.
   Example: 1. Tumbling and acrobatic skills
            2. Dance moves
            3. Variation in tempo
3. Floor exercise is performed to music in a 40' by 40' (12 meter by 12 meter) area.

COLLEGE LEVEL—PHYSICAL EDUCATION MAJOR STUDENTS

Since physical education majors are being trained for the teaching profession, they should be able to analyze and evaluate students' performance, along with having the ability to perform at least the basic skills for each sport. Therefore, the questions should be developed to evaluate their ability to comprehend and analyze movement, along with simple recall ability of facts and principles.

Tumbling
1. In order to initiate movement one must:
   a. Move the center of gravity upward of the base of support
   b. Displace the center of gravity past the base of support
   c. Shift the center of gravity to the lower limbs
   d. Tilt the head forward
2. When correcting a backward roll that was performed crooked, which of the following suggestions would *not* most likely be made?
   a. Keep the right elbow straight
   b. Do not turn the head to the side
   c. Push with the hands equally and simultaneously
   d. Push with the hands and feet simultaneously
3. Which of the following principles is *not* involved with the mechanics of executing the front handspring?
   a. Arms remaining overhead until landing
   b. Strong push action of the forward foot after the hurdle.
   c. Head kept in normal position throughout entire skill
   d. Legs meeting while in the inverted position

Vaulting
1. The most common reason for hitting the horse with the knees when attempting a squat vault is:
   a. Bringing knees to chest too late
   b. Poor hurdle
   c. Landing flat-footed on the board
   d. Leaning forward from the board on takeoff
2. When do the hips pass over the horse in non-layout vaults?
   a. Directly beneath the shoulders
   b. Before the shoulders
   c. After the shoulders
   d. None of the above
3. Common faults of the beginning vaulter include all but one of the following.
   a. Failure to use the board quickly
   b. Executing a hurdle that is too high
   c. Reaching the horizontal position in preflight
   d. Leaning forward when contacting the reuther board

Uneven Bars
1. The most common mistake beginners make in performing a back hip pullover on the low bar is:.
   a. Insufficient kick
   b. Allowing hips to move forward of the bar
   c. Forcing the head back as the legs kick
   d. Allowing the arms to extend
2. Why is it essential to bring the body back to the bar in an arched position from the cast preceding a back hip circle?
   a. To keep the shoulders upright
   b. To develop short axis rotation

   c. To ensure a tighter wrap

   d. To keep the arms from bending

3. The most common error made by beginners on the cast is:

   a. Keeping the arms straight

   b. Using a forward grip

   c. Allowing the shoulders to move back of the bar

   d. Piking as the body contacts the bar

Balance Beam

1. When spotting the backward roll, where does the spotter place her hands?

   a. On the hip area

   b. One hand on the abdomen, the other on the lower back

   c. One hand on the thigh, other hand on the arms

   d. Both hands around waist and upper hip area

2. Considering the mechanical action of the mounts below, which could not be easily transferred to another event in gymnastics?

   a. Straddle

   b. Squat

   c. Knee

   d. Wolf

3. When performing on the beam, one should be concerned with proper body alignment for which of the following reasons?

   a. So that skills may be performed in a mechanically correct manner

   b. For aesthetic beauty

   c. For ease of maneuverability

   d. So the spotter will not have to assist

Miscellaneous—Organization question

1. You are teaching gymnastics to fifty students in half a gym (30′ by 50′). There are four activities going on simultaneously. Which of the following arrangements of apparatus would be best for the situation? Consider skills being performed and amount of space needed for various skills on each apparatus, and remember that students will rotate as a group from one activity to the next. Rotation will be counter clockwise.

   b—Apparatus arranged so there is sufficient room for mounts, dismounts, landing in vaulting, and mat arrangement around the apparatus. Also it is arranged so that students will not use the same muscle groups from one event to the other.

a   b   c   d

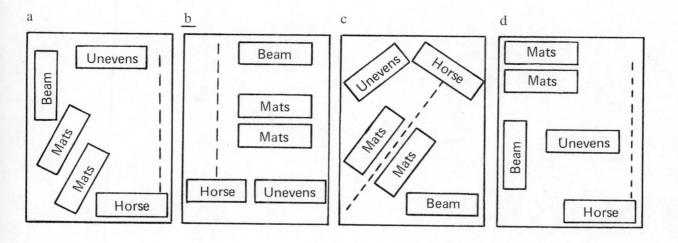

NOTES

CHAPTER NINE
ORGANIZING AND DIRECTING
A GYMNASTIC MEET

A meet that appears to be running smoothly is the result of many hours of preparation. Many first meets are very hectic, take hours to complete, and leave those in charge with a negative attitude towards future gymnastic meets. Therefore, it is hoped that the following information will serve as a guideline when you are asked to organize, direct, and/or sponsor a gymnastic meet at your school or club.

Planning a Gymnastic Meet

APPOINT COMMITTEES

1. Publicity
2. Equipment and supplies
3. Ticket sales: finances
4. Facilities
   a. Secure gym
   b. Secure locker room facilities—make sure there are adequate dressing and showering facilities
5. Committee to secure officials
6. Personnel to establish system for identifying the competitors
7. Hostesses
8. Awards committee
9. Committee for meals and/or lodging facilities (if necessary)

EVENTS FOR WOMEN

1. Individual events
   a. Balance beam
   b. Uneven parallel bars
   c. Side horse vaulting
   d. Floor exercise
   e. All around—individuals competing in all four events
2. Special events
   a. Tumbling
   b. Trampoline

PLACE

The gymnasium where the meet is to be held should meet the following criteria.
1. Be large enough to accomodate equipment used.
   a. 80 feet for vaulting (could be less), 60 feet for the runway, and 10 feet for landing beyond the horse. (Judges should be situated far enough from the four corners of the horse to get a clear view.)

b. 45 feet by 45 feet for floor exercise, allowing ample room for judges to be seated at each corner.
2. Have adequate light and proper temperature control. A cooler gym is preferable. Apparatus should be placed so there will not be any glare from the lights or sun.
3. Be large enough to accomodate spectators if there are to be any. In many cases it is advisable to rope off safety areas for gymnasts with signs stating "No Spectators Allowed Beyond This Point!"
4. Be free of hazards where gymnasts must perform and await their turn before performing.
    1. Buckled floors
    2. Projections from walls
    3. Excessive dust
    4. Unnecessary extension cords from the tape recorder or public address system.
5. Should have adequate electrical fixtures or outlets for tape recorders, public address systems, and record players.

TIME

The time of the meet will depend on many things. However, if it is possible to select a time, consider the following.
1. Number of entrants expected.
2. Age of gymnasts.
3. Traveling time involved to and from the meet.
4. Try to avoid having the meet too close to a meal unless the number of entrants is so great that you have no other choice.
5. Allow at least the following period of time per performer:
    a. Beam—three minutes (judging time included)
    b. Bars—one and a half to two minutes
    c. Vaulting—two minutes
    d. Floor exercise—three minutes
6. Consider time for moving equipment, warm-up periods, intermission, judges conferences, and presentation of awards.

DATE

Try to select a date well enough in advance so there will be few or no conflicts.

ENTRIES

Notices of meet and entry blanks should be sent out well in advance. They should contain information pertinent to the meet with any special regulations. An entry form and meet notice should contain the following.
1. Type of meet
    a. Optional
    b. Compulsory (stating which compulsories will be used)
    c. Age group
    d. Open (to anyone)
    e. Closed (usually a dual or district meet)
2. Date
3. Location
4. Time (time warm-ups start and time meet starts)
5. Sponsor
6. Sanction—if meet has to be sanctioned
7. Events
8. Fee per event, if any

9. Closing date for entries
10. Award system, if any
11. Notice that a physical examination is required before an individual will be allowed to compete.
12. Notice that the sponsoring organization will not be responsible for accidents incurred during the meet.
13. The entry blank portion should contain the following.
    a. Place for name, address, age, number (if any), and affiliation (school or club)
    b. Events to be held with a check space
    c. Place for gymnast's signature
    d. Place for coach's signature and parent's signature if the performer is a minor

Sample notice of meet

WOMEN'S OPEN OPTIONAL GYMNASTIC MEET

April 14, 19??

POOLESVILLE HIGH SCHOOL

POOLESVILLE, MARYLAND

<u>Sponsor</u> - Poolesville High School Gymnastic Club

<u>Place</u> - Women's gymnasium

<u>Time</u> - Warm-ups 9:00 a.m.

      Meet 10:00 a.m.

<u>Events</u> - Floor exercise, balance beam, side horse vaulting, uneven parallel bars, and all around

<u>Entry fee</u> - $1.00 per event - $5.00 for All Around

<u>Deadline</u> - Entries close with the meet director, Mrs. Bertha Stevens, on Monday, April 10, at 4:00 p.m.

<u>Awards</u> - Trophies will be given to the first three places in each event and the top three All Around.

Detach the entry below and return to meet director

WOMEN'S OPEN OPTIONAL GYMNASTIC MEET

April 14, 19??

Poolesville High School   Poolesville, Maryland

Name _____ Age _____ Registration No. _____

Address _____
                Street   City   State   Zip Code

School or club affiliation _____

Events: Check those you wish to enter:

___ Floor Ex. _____ Beam _____ Bars _____ Vaulting _____ All Around.

Total fee remitted: $ _____ (@ $1.00 per event; All Around $5.00)

Note: I understand that the school will not be responsible for any
      injuries incurred during participation in this meet.

                    Gymnast's signature _____

                    Coach's signature _____

                    Parent's signature _____

Sample group entry form

WOMEN'S OPEN OPTIONAL GYMNASTIC MEET

APRIL 14, 19??

SARASOTA SPRINGS HIGH SCHOOL

SARASOTA, MARYLAND

Name	Age	Reg. No.	Club	Beam	Bars	Vaulting	Fl. Ex	AA	Fee
Cindy Claggett	19	486	Holoke	x	x	x	x	x	$5.00
Linda Gottshall	19	65	Holoke	x		x			$2.00
Ellen Babuska	19	876	Holoke	x		x			$2.00

Total remittance $9.00

Note: I understand that the school will not be responsible for any
injuries incurred during participation in this meet.

Coach's signature _____

AWARDS

Decide on quantity, quality, cost, design, etc., and order well in advance. Order extras in case of ties.

OFFICIALS

The number in parentheses will indicate the ideal number needed for an event or meet. If two or more events are held simultaneously, the number will increase accordingly.

a. Meet director (1)
b. Judges (5). This is the ideal situation, but two judges per event are adequate for local meets.
c. Scorers (2)
d. Flashers (one per event)
e. Runners (2)
f. Announcer (1)
g. Timer (1)

DUTIES OF THE OFFICIALS

a. *Meet director*
   1. Responsible for conducting the meet in an orderly fashion.
   2. Must be available to answer questions that may arise in various situations.
   3. Handles protests if any. In school or club situations, the governing body usually decides how the protests are to be handled.
   4. Makes decisions on matters not covered by the rules.
b. *Superior judge* (included as one of the five judges mentioned above)
   1. Score performances.
   2. Make sure that the range of the other judges scores are within legal limits.
   3. Call conferences if she feels that the performer has not been given a realistic score.
   4. Make sure that the judges are in the proper places and alert.
c. *Judges*
   1. Score performers to the best of their ability.
   2. Make notations when scoring so they are able to defend scores in case of protest.
   3. Be alert and in the proper place.
d. *Scorers*
   1. Sit at the head table and keep a master copy of all scores for all events.
   2. Record scores accurately.
e. *Flasher*
   Sit beside superior judge. After scores have been turned into the head (superior) judge and they are within limits, the flasher will then by some method show the performers and audience the *average* score given by the judges.
f. *Runners*
   Stand or sit beside judge. Take score to superior judge as quickly as possible after performance.
g. *Announcer*
   1. Give all directions (loudly and clearly).
   2. Inform competitors of events, warm-ups, and the line up.
   3. Should have enough knowledge of gymnastics to inform competitors and audience of rulings or incidents that may happen and to inform audience about nature of composition of the routines they are watching.
   4. Announce the results after they have been checked and approved by the director.
h. *Timers*
   Time the floor exercise and balance beam routines to make sure they are within the time limit.

i. *Other personnel*
1. Physician or nurse
2. Guides or hostesses
3. Ticket takers
4. Equipment movers
5. Persons to organize contestants
6. Electrician (optional)
7. Photographer (optional)

Note: If any of the officials besides the judges are to be paid for their services, this should be decided in advance. Checks should be ready to issue immediately after the meet is completed. A budget, including gate receipts and fees for registration, should be kept. If at all possible, meets should be self-supporting.

Organization and Direction

SETTING UP EQUIPMENT

After entries are closed and the judges have been obtained, it is advisable to design some type of plan for setting up and moving equipment. Arrangements must be made to fit the needs of the gymnasts and other personnel involved. If it is at all possible, it is best to have all equipment set up for a warm-up period to allow the performers to adjust to the particular pieces of apparatus being used before the meet begins. If this is not feasible, then the gymnasts should be given a longer time to warm-up on the apparatus when it is set up.

If only one event is to be running at a time, the following order is suggested.

1. Floor exercise
2. Vaulting
3. Beam
4. Bars

or

1. Vaulting
2. Bars
3. Beam
4. Floor exercise

The floor exercise mat (or area if mat is not available) should be set up in advance to make sure it flattens out as much as possible.

For the warm-up period, the floor patterns could be as shown to the right.

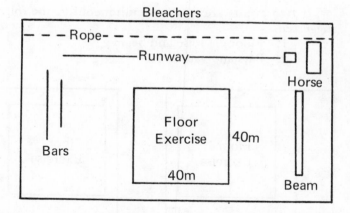

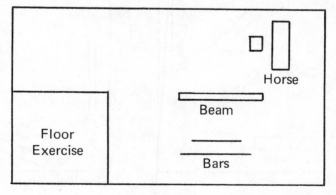

After the warm-up period leave equipment where it is or put the horse, beam and bars on transporters ready to move. After floor exercise is completed, have designated persons roll up the mat while others are ready to move horse and mats into position either on a diagonal or to the side of the gym. After vaulting, if the horse was moved, put it in original position or take to storage room, and move both bars and beam with mats to the center of the gym, leaving ample room for mount, dismount, and judges seats.

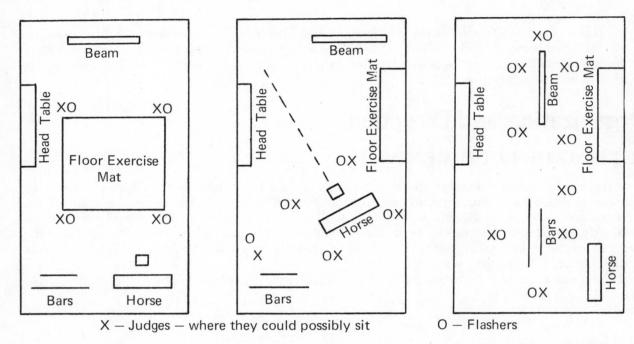

X — Judges — where they could possibly sit   O — Flashers

If two events are to run simultaneously, the following order of events and setup of apparatus is suggested.
1. Floor exercise and beam
2. Bars and vaulting

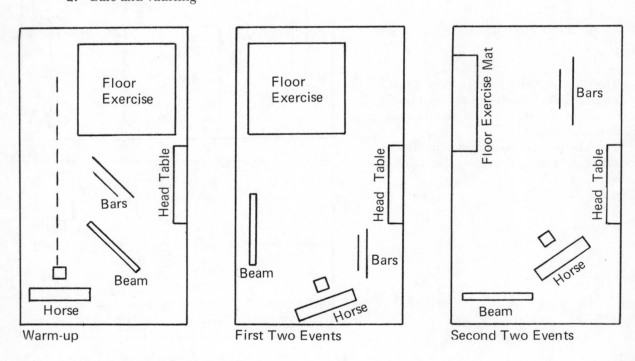

Warm-up   First Two Events   Second Two Events

If two events are running simultaneously, the sponsor and meet director must be prepared to decide for a gymnast if she is called to both events simultaneously. What usually happens in this case is that the gymnast selects the event to perform in first and is then either given sufficient time to rest before performing the other event or is placed at the bottom of the list.

It is also advisable to have a person responsible for making sure the performers are ready when called "on deck" (next up) or "in the hole" (third up). In meets where there are many entrants, this person should line the performers up and not allow them to wander around.

SELECTING ORDER OF PERFORMERS

After entries are in, make a list of all performers in each event. Doing one event at a time, place their names in some type of container, and as you draw them out, make up the official list. A performer should not go first or last in more than one event.

SCORE SHEETS

After drawing names for order of performances, make up score sheets for the judges, scorers, and, if possible, extras for the coaches and contestants.

Sample score sheet:

WOMEN'S OPEN MEET

APRIL 14, 19??

HULABOO HIGH

Judge's signature _____ (Alice Cox) _____

Event ____ (Beam) ____   Judge's number _____ (3) _____

Scores

Name	No.	Judge 1	Judge 2	Judge 3	Judge 4	Judge 5	Average	Place
Ramsay, Bobby	42			6.2				
Cooper, Phyllis	101			5.8				
Garvey, Pat	68			7.6				
Moser, Lorraine	7			6.5				
Shifflett, Charlotte	14			7.2				

Note: This particular type of score sheet can be used by each judge (as is done here), as well as used by the scorer for the master sheet. If extras were passed out to the audience, they can keep score, also.

FLASH CARDS

If commercial flash cards cannot be purchased, they can be made out of oil cloth or cardboard and can be attached to rings so they can be flipped. There should be one complete set for each flasher and a set with three rows of numbers for the head judge's flasher so the average score can be shown. Cards made for diving could also be used. An opaque projector could be used to flash groups of scores.

MISCELLANEOUS EQUIPMENT AND MATERIALS NEEDED

Typewriter for head table
Tables and chairs for scorers and announcer
Desks or chairs for flashers and judges
Adding machine
Microphone
Scratch paper for judges and scorers
Pencils
Clipboards
Chalk—magnesium
Stop watches
Resin
Tape recorder
Piano
Rope—to rope off vaulting runway and to keep spectators out of gym area
Tape—measuring tape to measure vaulting distances and check dimensions of equipment (height etc., if necessary), adhesive tape for gymnasts if needed
Sand or emery paper to remove chalk from bars
Extension cords
Magic markers to make signs
Mop or broom to remove excessive chalk dust from floor
First aid supplies
Record player

GENERAL JUDGING PROCEDURES

New judging rules and routine requirements for women's gymnastics were instituted prior to the 1968 Olympics. General changes are discussed below; however, for specific deductions please consult the USGF Interpretations of the International Rules for Women's Gymnastics. (May be obtained from USGF, PO Box 4699, Tucson, Arizona 85717.)

Five women judges rate all exercises. The score of the head judge is not used unless there is a conference when scores are out of range or when the head judge feels the gymnast has been improperly scored. The judges will confer on the first exercise of each event (except finals), then arrive at the remaining scores independently. Of the four scores obtained, they are first approved by the head judge, then the low and high are eliminated and the remaining two are averaged. *Only the averaged score is flashed to the audience and performers.*

The difference between the middle scores should not exceed the following:
.3 if the scores are between 9.5 and 10.0
.5 if the scores are between 8.5 and 9.45
1.0 in all other cases
In finals, differences between scores should not exceed the following:
.2 if the scores are between 9.5 and 10.0
.3 if the scores are between 8.5 and 9.45
.5 if the scores are between 7.0 and 8.45
1.0 in all other cases

COMPULSORY EXERCISES (MAY NOT BE REPEATED)

Compulsory exercises may receive a maximum of 10.0 points. They are awarded in the following manner.

Balance beam, floor exercise, and unevens
- 2.0 Exactness and correctness of the exercise
- .5 Exactness of direction and of the floor pattern
- 1.5 Exactness of rhythm
- 1.0 Elegance of gymnast
- 1.5 Sureness of execution
- 1.5 Amplitude
- 1.0 Coordination of movements
- 1.0 Lightness of jumps and acrobatics

Compulsory vault
- 2.0 Preflight
- 2.0 On horse—push-off
- 2.0 Afterflight
- 2.0 Stretch of body (body position)
- .5 Direction of vault
- 1.5 General balance of vault

Note: For detailed information consult the FIG Code of Points for women or the USGF Interpretations of the International Rules for Women's Gymnastics.

OPTIONAL EXERCISES

Optional exercises may receive a maximum of 10.0 points. They are awarded in the following manner.

Balance beam, floor exercise, and unevens
- 4.0 points difficulty (2 superior elements—1 point each; 4 medium elements—.5 point each)
- 1.5 points originality and value of the combinations of the exercise
- .5 points general value of exercise composition
- 1.5 points execution
- 1.5 points amplitude
- 1.0 point general impression

The optional horse vault will be made known to the judges prior to execution. Breakdown depends upon original value of vaults. Various deductions will be made for not meeting the preflight, on horse, and afterflight and landing requirements of that particular vault called.

Code- 1. 4.0-Diff.
2. 1.5-Orig. & Combinations
3. 0.5-Gen Composition Value
4. 1.5-Execution
5. 1.5-Amplitude
6. 1.0-Gen. Impression

EVENT Floor Exercise

Competitor   Remarks
Name or
Number   Diff.   Exec.Breaks-Falls   Orig.& Comb.   1. ____
                                                             2. ____
                                                             3. ____
                                                             4. ____
                                                             5. ____
                                                             6. ____

                                                        Final Score ____

                    Remarks   1. ____
                                                         2. ____
                                                         3. ____
                                                         4. ____
                                                         5. ____
                                                         6. ____

                                                        Final Score ____

                    Remarks   1. ____
                                                         2. ____
                                                         3. ____
                                                         4. ____
                                                         5. ____
                                                         6. ____

                                                        Final Score ____

                    Remarks   1. ____
                                                         2. ____
                                                         3. ____
                                                         4. ____
                                                         5. ____
                                                         6. ____

                                                        Final Score ____

                    Remarks   1. ____
                                                         2. ____
                                                         3. ____
                                                         4. ____
                                                         5. ____
                                                         6. ____

                                                        Final Score ____

Note: By using a scoring method similar to the one above a judge can jot down many remarks concerning the performance which she can later refer to if necessary. It is also wise to note names of elements of difficulty and other important comments about combinations, use of areas, amplitude, etc.

NOTES

NOTES

Glossary

1. Aerial—Body suspended in air; performance of skill without hands, with the body usually in an arched position.
2. Arched—The back is hyperextended, shoulders relaxed and back, and abdomen forward.
3. A terre—On the floor.
4. Backbend (bridge)—Hands and feet support body while in arched position on floor. Head is tilted up and back. Back is facing floor.
5. Bent hip ascent—A position in vaulting where the body pikes in preflight, then continues with the remainder of the vault.
6. Crotch seat (straddle seat)—Beam: one leg on each side of beam, sitting facing either end. Bars: same as stride position, one leg in front of the bar, the other leg behind the bar. On the bars this position is rarely referred to as the straddle seat.
7. Dégagé—To remove or disengage.
8. Downbackward—Moving arms down to side of body, past the side of the body, then backward and upward.
9. Ectomorph—The extreme ectomorphic individual is slender and frail looking, with a large forehead, small face, and a sharp nose. She tends to have a slender neck, narrow chest, flat abdomen, and long thin limbs.
10. En dedans—Movement rearward to front position.
11. En dehors—Movement from the front to the back.
12. Endomorph—The extreme endomorphic individual has rounded contours, a predominance of weight in the abdominal, hip, and thigh area, and short thick limbs.
13. English handstand—Beam: handstand done facing the length of the beam; heels of hands together.
14. En l'air—In the air.
15. Flank—Raising the hips as high as possible and keeping the supporting arm straight, lift both legs together and straight up and over the apparatus. As legs move over apparatus, lift nonsupporting arm.
16. Flip—Movement performed without hands. Body position in air is tucked.
17. Foreupward—Move arms from side of body to a forward and upward position, stopping at a 45° angle.
18. Front support—Beam or bars: upper thighs resting on beam or bar with arms straight, shoulders extended, head up.
19. Inverted—Head down, legs extended upward. Example: headstand.
20. Jeté—Small hop.
21. Layout—Straight body ascent vault: as hands contact the horse, the body is completely straight and should be at least on a 45° angle to the horse. Tumbling: refers to an aerial position where the body is completely extended (slightly arched) while suspended in air. Movement usually revolves around the head in layout movement.
22. Long hang—Bars: hands in a forward grip, body straight and hanging from the high bar.
23. Mesomorph—The extreme mesomorphic individual has a heavy angular outline with thick massive muscles. Her bones are prominent; the neck is long and strong; the chest is large; the waist is long and slender; and the limbs are muscular.
24. Pike—Hips flexed but legs straight and together.
25. Plié—Bending the knees. The feet may be in any of the ballet positions. Knees turn out over toes.
26. "Pop"—Bars: refers to the movement of the eagle catch and hecht dismount. This movement is a very explosive one in that upper and lower body forcefully move up and back simultaneously.

27. Prone—Lying, usually on the floor or mat, full length with the face downward. This position is used for exercises such as the push-up.
28. Punch—Forcefully spring from the mat or board with slight knee bend to get maximum lift. The movement must be rapid and hard.
29. Rear arch (supine arch)—Supporting the body weight on the hands and heels. Back bend could also be referred to as a supine arch.
30. Rear sitting—Sitting on, but having back to apparatus. Example: sitting on low bar with back to high bar.
31. Semi-plié—Slight knee bend.
32. Single leg flank—Moving one leg through the flank position.
33. Split—One leg extended forward, other leg extended backward with buttocks and legs flat on floor. Upper body facing toward forward leg. Trunk may be arched backward, bent over forward leg, or held erect.
34. Squat—Tumbling: knees are brought to the chest. Jumping: heels are raised to the buttocks.
35. "Stick"—Vaulting: landing without having to step forward, sideward, or backward to gain balance.
36. Stoop—Upper body flexed, legs straight and together.
37. Straddle—Position in which the legs are separated sideways. Upper body may be erect or flexed, may be sitting or standing, or used in air as position in vaulting, beam, or bar work.
38. Stride—Bars: one leg extended forward of the bar, other leg in back of the bar; sitting on the bar or supported by the hands. Running: refers to length of steps.
39. Supine—Lying on back, facing upward.
40. Swan—Bars: body arched and balanced on the upper thighs. Arms overhead or obliquely sideways. Vaulting: same as hecht, going over horse with body in arched position, face down.
41. Tendu—Snapping one foot to the other foot.
42. Tour—Turn.
43. Tuck—Knees bent and close to the chest. Examples: tuck jump and position in air for front or back flip.

Skills with Multiple Names

TUMBLING

1. Forward roll—front roll
2. Headstand—head balance
3. Handstand—hand balance
4. Front limbre—front over
5. Tip-up—knee elbow stand—turk stand—frog hand balance
6. Somersault—sommie—flip—aerial (Refer to glossary for clarification, as these terms are used incorrectly in many instances.)
7. Back roll extension—back roll to handstand snap down
8. Snap down—mule kick—handstand snap down to stoop
9. Back handspring—flip flop
10. Tinsica—mounter

BALANCE BEAM

1. Straddle seat—crotch seat
2. V seat—V sit—balanced seat—piked seat
3. Step on mount—one leg squat mount
4. Arabesque—scale
5. Windy—kick through handstand making half turn on one arm to stand
6. English handstand dismount—handstand snapdown dismount

UNEVEN PARALLEL BARS

1. Cast from high bar to hip circle on low—flying hip circle—cast rotate from high to low—cast wrap
2. Single leg stem rise—single leg kip to high
3. Mill circle—stride leg rotate—crotch circle
4. Stride support—split support
5. Cast—push away

Note: There are many other skills with multiple names, however, the above are most frequently disputed.

Additional Resource Materials

BOOKS

1. Allison, June. *Advanced Gymnastics for Women*. London: Stanley Paul and Co., Ltd., 1963 (U.S. Distributor, "Sportshelf").
2. Drury, Blanche and Andrea Schmid. *Gymnastics for Women*. Palo Alto, California: The National Press, 1964.
3. Frederick, A. Bruce. *Women's Gymnastics*. Physical Education Activities Series. Dubuque, Iowa: Wm. C. Brown Company, 1966.
4. Leinert, Walter. *The Modern Girl Gymnast on the Uneven Parallel Bars*. Indianapolis: The Author (1010 West 64th Street, Indianapolis, Indiana), 1957.
5. Prchal, Mildred. *Artistic Gymnastics—Floor Exercise*. Waldwick, New Jersey: Hoctor Dance Records, Inc. (Distributor), 1964.
6. Kaywell, Grace. *Ballet for Gymnastics*. Santa Monica, California: Sunby Publication, P.O. Box 777, 1965.
7. Takemoto, Masao. *Illustrated Women's Gymnastics*. (U.S. Distributor, Frank Endo, 12200 South Berendo, Los Angeles, California 90044).

PERIODICALS

1. *Amateur Athletic Union Gymnastics Handbook*. AAU Office, 231 West 38th Street, New York, New York 10018.
2. *DGWS Gymnastics Guide*. June 1971–June 1973. Division for Girls and Women's Sports of the American Association for Health, Physical Education and Recreation, 1201 16th Street N.W., Washington, D.C. 20036.
3. *F.I.G. Code of Points*. AAU Office, 231 West 38th Street, New York, New York 10018.
4. *Modern Gymnast*. P.O. Box 611, Santa Monica, California 90406.
5. *U.S.G.F. Age Group Gymnastic Workbook*. 1964. P.O. Box 4699, Tucson, Arizona 85202.
6. *U.S. Gymnast*. P.O. Box 53, Iowa City, Iowa 52240.

VISUAL AIDS

FILMS

1. *Gymnastics (Motivational film)*—very fundamental. DGWS. 1201 16th Street N.W., Washington, D.C. 20036.
2. *Women's Gymnastics—Beam and Bars*. Muriel Grossfeld. Club 15, BBD&O 383 Madison Avenue, New York, New York 10017.
3. Frank Endo. 12200 South Berendo, Los Angeles, California 90044. Has film of Olympic games and World Championships.

OTHER AIDS

Frederick, A. Bruce. *Gymnastic Action Cards*, Minneapolis: Burgess Publishing Co. 1965.

FLOOR EXERCISE RECORDS

Music for Floor Exercise I & II. Directed by Phyllis Cooper. Pianist, Katherine Terhune. Available from TurCo, 19 North Greenwood Avenue, Hopewell, New Jersey 08525.
Hoctor Record Company, Inc. Waldwick, New Jersey 07463.
    Carries several selections.

Index

250